ENCYCLOPEDIA FOR THE BETRAYED

Your Essential A - Z Guide for Anyone Who's Ever Been Lied To, Cheated On and Left for Dead

ELLE GRANT

ISBN 978-1-7753898-0-4

ISBN 978-1-7753898-1-1 (ebook)

ISBN 978-1-7753898-2-8 (other digital)

Credits for cover design: Marilyn Mets/Blue Sky Studio

Printed in the United States of America

Visit betrayedwivesclub.blogspot.com

Created with Vellum

Foreword

Close to a decade ago, when I had just discovered that my husband was having an affair, I hadn't a clue how I was going to survive. The pain was so intense, my world so shattered, that I could barely breathe. I had three young children. I had an about-to-be-published book. I had a mother dying in the hospital. And I had a husband who had cheated on me.

What I didn't have was a network of women who could support me until I could find solid ground beneath my feet. I didn't have the wisdom of those who'd been there and survived. I scoured bookstores, both bricks-and-mortar and online. I Googled. I raised my antennae for any hint that others in my orbit had experienced what I was going through. For the most part, I came up empty.

I swung wildly between hope for my marriage and utter despair. I felt cut off from the rest of the world with no idea who I could trust with my secret. And I felt profoundly alone in my pain.

It took me well over a year, during which I buried my beautiful mother and somehow promoted a book, to believe that I was going to survive this. That I even *wanted* to survive it. And another year before I could imagine staying in my marriage even though I finally felt strong enough to leave.

And within those two years, I began to imagine a space where betrayed women could gather and share our stories.

I believe in the power of storytelling to heal. I believe that when we own our stories, we control our destinies. I believe that laughter and tears are alchemy that can heal anything. And I believe that the most powerful words in the universe are "me too."

These beliefs coalesced to become Betrayed Wives Club, a blog where I slowly started telling my own story. It was a thrill when my blog stats revealed I had one reader. Then two, then three. Slowly, over months, more betrayed wives found the site. And slowly, they began to share their own stories.

Reporters found me and featured my story in the pages of magazines and newspapers. More betrayed wives came. Maybe even you came.

Our stories echoed each other even if the circumstances were different. I realized that infidelity really is excruciating. It wasn't just me overreacting. And it's something that our culture rarely talks about with nuance or compassion.

Except those of us in Betrayed Wives Club. We talk about everything – from the agony of finding out to the fear of it happening again to the confusion of whether to stay or go to the bittersweet bliss of rebuilding a marriage to the realization that the marriage is truly over.

We cry. We rant. Most surprising of all, we laugh. A lot.

Betrayed Wives Club is the site I wish had existed when I was desperate for help. Encyclopedia for the Betrayed is the book version, the guidebook I wished I'd found on the shelves. Let it be yours.

This book includes the wisdom and compassion of the women who've come to Betrayed Wives Club and laid bare their hearts, who've trusted me with their stories, who've healed when they couldn't imagine it was possible, and who've grown stronger...and then used that strength to support other secret sisters reeling from their new reality.

I dedicate this book to you and to my mother, who never flinched from my pain but instead held me close, confident in my heart's ability to heal.

You Are Here

•

Yes, you are here. And I know how disorienting that is. I know that, just yesterday it seems, you were picking up your kids from school and listening to their chatter of the day, or you were cutting the tops off strawberries and putting them in a pretty bowl, you were wondering whether to order those cute shoes online, you were noticing how prominent the veins on your mother's aging hands have become or the lines newly etched at the corners of your own eyes.

And then. You discovered a text, or picked up a call, or overheard a conversation. So now you're here. Reeling. Frightened. Lost.

Let me make a promise: You won't be here forever, not in this place of abject terror, red-hot fury, stunned shock and confusion. You will inch forward, like an injured bird. You will pick up speed as you heal. And you will arrive at a place you can scarcely imagine right now. Not over it, exactly. But through it.

Millions of us have survived this. And more than surviving, we have emerged with our hearts still open, our integrity unshaken, our humour intact. You can too.

But for now: You Are Here. Let's get you oriented:

How to answer the question: How are you?

Fine, thank you.

Doing okay. How about you?

A bit stressed, thanks for asking.

Barely holding it together. Please pray for me.

Really? You really want to know?

Unintelligible due to convulsive sobbing

What to take to feel better:

Ibuprofen or acetaminophen for that motherf#$@%*er of a headache

A glass of wine (one. And only one.)

SSRIs or other prescription medication, under a doctor's supervision.

A lit match to his clothes

An axe to his laptop

A financial retainer to your lawyer

Popular Nicknames for the Other Woman

Bitch

Fucking bitch

Two-bit whore

Bitchy McBitchface

Ho-worker

Homewrecker

Sexatary

Your girlfriend (said in your best 13-year-old mean-girl taunt)

Things To Eat When You Don't Think You Can Eat (see also Eat, What To)

Ensure or other meal replacement drink (Ed. note: tequila is NOT a meal replacement drink)

Soup

Crackers

Cereal

Smoothies

Entire chocolate cheesecake

Common Infidelity Acronyms

OW: Other Woman

D-Day: Discovery/Disclosure Day

OC: Other Child

NPD: Narcissistic Personality Disorder

SA: Sex Addict or Sex Addiction

AP: Affair Partner

WH: Wayward Husband (though 'wayward' sounds entirely too quaint)

CS: Cheating Spouse

Healthy Habits To Keep You Sane

Meditation (pretty much just breathing while you think about breathing)

Exercise — whatever gets you moving and no, walking the halls in your bathrobe while you ring your hands and moan doesn't count

Talking to a trusted friend (see **Who To Tell**)

Writing in a journal (see **Journaling**)

Walking in the woods (see **Nature**)

Hobbies (painting, music, furniture restoration, auto mechanics. Anything that takes you out of your pain and into a place where you forget yourself.)

Excuses To Give Your Boss When You Can't Come Into Work

I have the flu.

My kid has the flu.

I have a doctor's appointment.

I need a mental health day.

My life has become a country song and I'm channelling the lyrics.

Ummmm...is bail included in my employee benefits package?

The Best Advice From Betrayed Wives

"Get into therapy right away."

"This will become less a part of your life with time. That will be good enough to feel better, and you will be surprised by that just as I am."

"How can you get him to understand how painful this is? You don't; he doesn't have the capacity to empathize with your pain because he warped his thinking into justifying this behavior in the first place. But he can try... and that will be enough to feel better, I promise."

"I waited to file for divorce until I had given him a chance to change, but spent that time figuring out exactly how I felt and what I wanted regardless of whether he was able to. I came to terms with the fact that I no longer wanted a life with him regardless of what he did or didn't do around the same time I found out he was still cheating. It made walking away easier and so freeing."

"Make therapy a condition of continuing the marriage and living arrangements. I made it a condition of me giving him a chance, but we were still separated for a year until I was ready to be around him."

"Don't email or text anybody in the middle of the night or when you've had less than six hours of sleep."

"You don't have to have this all figured out today."

"Exercise. Just get out and move."

"You can never un-tell somebody. Be careful who you tell."

"Don't make any permanent decisions until you feel more stable."

"Take care of yourself first. Get out for nature walks daily. It will help release your pain."

"Take it one day at a time. I decided within the first two weeks that I would give it a year as long as my sexually addicted spouse did not view porn, masturbate or pay for sex. That was the line I drew for any possible hope for the marriage."

"I felt rushed to decide whether I would stay or go, rushed to know if our marriage would survive, rushed to decide if i could forgive. And in the midst of trying to make all these decisions, I was rushing my healing, which I know now can't be done. It takes time."

"I took care of ME first. Every day I got stronger and had a little more clarity than the day before."

"My best friend reminded me that I was the victim, the OW was not as the OW knew of me before their affair started. My friend also told me not to leave, which was my first reaction, so I could think clearly before I reacted."

"Do NOT contact the Other Woman. It won't give you the satisfaction you want."

"Get tested for STDs."

"Tell yourself that you will survive. I willed myself to envision a time where I wouldn't be in constant agony even if I couldn't trust that would be true."

"When the possibility of seeing the OW at a party was very real, Elle gave me words to say in the event of a confrontation: 'I have nothing to say to you.' I rehearsed it over and over."

"'My heartbreak, my rules.' I read that on Betrayed Wives Club in the early days and haven't let it go. It speaks to our vulnerability and our empowerment – both essential to recovery from betrayal."

"Take care of yourself because you are strong and beautiful and lovable. Take it one day, one hour, one minute at a time."

"Use an herbal or over-the-counter sleep aid or see your doctor. Please dear sister, get some rest. Also do your best not to drink alcohol. It does not help and puts you at risk of unhelpful choices."

"When I didn't know which way was up, down, to run or sit idle: Elle said 'just show up, that's it' and it took pressure off."

A

Adultery, How to Survive (see also Betrayal)

So. Your husband has committed what is clinically and sanitarily known as adultery, though, except for the sex part, there doesn't seem to be much that's "adult" about it. It's basically two kids playing "let's pretend." Regardless, it's devastating. More devastating than most of us imagined.

My experience with adultery began when I was nine. My mother got a phone call from a man reporting that his wife was having an affair with my father. This led my mother to drinking. A lot. For years. Thank goodness for AA is all I can say.

None of this is to say that your husband's adultery or affair will necessarily lead to you becoming an alcoholic or addict. However, AA, or any of the 12-step groups, offers an amazing blueprint for how to live your life. In a nutshell: Realize that there is much that is beyond your control. Take responsibility for what you can control. Surrender what you can't. Listen carefully and compassionately to people's stories. Healing is possible. But it takes work. And time.

Affair, Your Husband is Admitting An

Maybe you stumbled onto a piece of jewelry in his car that is definitely not yours. Maybe you found a text or an e-mail. Perhaps someone told you. Maybe he confessed. However you discovered your husband's affair, you're reeling.

What now? Well, the rules have changed. And he needs to know that. If he is telling you that he doesn't want to separate or divorce, then here are a few non-negotiables:

1. He must have absolutely NO CONTACT with the affair partner/OW. None. Nada. Nope. No "last meeting to say goodbye." No returning of gifts. No final texts to talk it over. Just a straightforward "I regret that I jeopardized my marriage and I am committed to trying to repair it. Going forward, there will be no contact between us." And then, it must be enforced. Your husband must ignore any overtures by her to restore contact. Texts must be deleted. Emails must be deleted. Phone calls must be ignored. You must also have No Contact: Block her. Mute her. Remove her from social media.
2. There must be total transparency between your partner and you. If he bumps into her, he must tell you. If she tries to contact him, he must tell you. If he slips and calls her, he must tell you. Any further secrets contribute to the destruction of your marriage and further erosion of trust.
3. Your marriage must be nurtured. Affairs are exciting because each affair partner is putting a whole lot of energy into them. From outfits to cologne to trysts, a lot of planning and plotting goes into every interaction. He must commit to

reinvesting that energy into your marriage, and you, in time, must do the same. It will feel awful because you hate his guts right now. It will feel awful because you will convince yourself that she was prettier or more interesting or wilder in bed. Surely she didn't nag at him the way you do. Or badger him for details. Maybe. Maybe not (you'd be shocked at how many of these Other Women are total nightmares). No matter. Each of you has to agree that you will work through this awful part to rebuild a marriage that's meaningful and emotionally safe and worth something to each of you.

Affirmations, Positive

When my youngest daughter was nine years old, she stuck Post-it notes around her room. On each was written something like "It's okay to make mistakes. You're human" and "You don't have to be perfect" and "You are fine just the way you are." She wrote one for me, which read:

You are strong.

You are brave.

You are talented.

You are beautiful.

Years later this tattered message is still taped to my mirror, where I read it each time I examine my wrinkles and my age spots. And here's the thing: Affirmations aren't just feel-good nonsense. Science tells us they work. "You're disgusting and nobody will ever love you again" simply can't coexist in the same brain at the same time as "you are beautiful and worthy of love."

Inspired by my daughter, I began replacing that critical

voice in my head – you know the one! – that chastised me for having thick thighs, for making a stupid remark to a friend. The voice that sometimes even said "No wonder he cheated on you." I replaced that inner critic with someone kinder. Someone who, when I catch a glimpse of myself getting out of the shower, says "wow, those legs look strong" or "that beautiful belly has been home to three babies" or "not bad for 50-plus." A voice that says "Healing is hard work. You're doing your best."

Antidepressants, The Power of

Growing up with a pill-popping mother who ultimately conquered an addiction to anti-anxiety meds (washed down with vodka) left me leery of any pill that promised a solution to anything. I was sure pills simply created more problems.

That, however, was then. I have since learned a whole lot more about mental health issues, trauma, PTSD, and brain chemistry, leading me to appreciate that treatment exists to help.

Antidepressants or anti-anxiety meds won't magically make you feel better. What they can do, properly prescribed and properly taken, is uncoil that knot in your stomach just a bit. They can keep you from killing yourself (see **Suicide**). They can keep you functioning at your job. They can help you parent. They are not a cure-all. You still have to do the work. But they can lift that boulder off your chest just enough that you might slip out from beneath it.

Anti-versaries

Cute name for a painful reminder. Anti-versaries are those dates that seem forever etched in our hearts, as if written with broken glass. They include but are not limited to:

D-Day: The date you learned your husband was cheating.

D-Day #2, 3 or 4: The dates you learned he was cheating again, or still cheating, or you learned new information about old cheating.

Your actual anniversary: The day you married this idiot.

Birthdays, family celebrations, trips: Anything that reminds you that "this time last year/two years ago/five years ago" life felt a whole lot different.

My anti-versary is December 10. That's the date I got the bitch-slap that is D-Day.

One year later, still married to my husband, I created an anti-versary tradition in order to pre-empt what I expected to be a brutal day of anger and sadness. My husband and I each took the day off work, hired a babysitter for our children, and drove a few hours away to a massive mall. There we spent the day holiday shopping for our family and each other. We had a long lunch that included wine. We laughed. I cried. We talked about what had happened one year before. It was, against all odds, a good day. And it taught me that we can write over memory.

The next year, we did the same thing. And the year after that. Now, more than a decade later, December 10 isn't D-Day so much as our annual holiday shopping day. We take the day off and have a long lunch somewhere out of town. We focus on each other and remind ourselves why we're still together. A day that would otherwise serve up reminders of betrayal and disappointment has transformed into a day about family and resilience and second chances. Not a day of reckoning but a day of recreation. Re-creation.

That's what we're doing, isn't it? We're re-creating our lives.

Whether you're still trying to rebuild a marriage with your partner or you're no longer with him, reclaim your anti-versary. Make it a day in which you celebrate what you have in your life, even if what you have right now is some dog-eared divorce papers and a bed.

Happy December 10 to all of you. Happy anti-versary.

Anger

I hated waking in the night to my parents fighting. The yelling. The thuds on the wall that divided our bedrooms. The slamming doors.

I hated the switch that would flip in my brother's eyes, when he would suddenly turn from the guy I adored to someone I feared. Once he battered me so badly that my mother suggested a trip to the ER but nobody was sober enough to take me.

So the calculus in my head goes like this: Anger = Chaos + Violence

In my world, if someone was angry, anything could happen. Marriages could go "poof." Friendships could dissolve. Brothers could betray. It could all fall apart.

I didn't want my childhood shaken. As long as nobody was angry, I could pretend that everything was fine. It wasn't, of course. My mother drank to quash her anger and hurt. My father drank to forget his frustration. My brother drank and smoked pot to numb his anger and confusion.

I raged.

But girls aren't supposed to be angry. And so I drank too. I drank my shame. And I drank my hurt. And I drank my disappointment and my fear. Mostly I drank my fury.

I learned to not rock the boat. Many nights alcohol allowed the wall I'd built around my feelings to dissolve just enough, and then my grief would pour out. Or someone would say something I took offence to, and my anger, grateful to have a target, would unleash.

I internalized a second equation: My Anger + Expression of it = Shame

And then I learned of my husband's cheating. I swung wildly between paralyzing emotional pain and a blazing fury that consumed me. I destroyed an expensive watch. I trashed a diamond necklace. I knocked a television set onto the floor. I threw a hot pizza at my husband. I felt crazy. I *was* crazy.

My anger spent, I felt empty, void of anything except a deep shame at my lack of control.

My therapist taught me how to feel my anger without breaking things. She taught me that my anger was legitimate, that it had something to teach me. She gave me a new equation:

Healthy Boundaries + Violation of Those Boundaries = Righteous Anger.

I started to pay attention to my anger before it consumed me. I tried to notice when I'd get that flicker of irritation because my husband said something, or did something, or didn't do something. I'd check in with myself: What was my anger telling me? Was I being disrespected? Taken for granted? Devalued?

Anger, my therapist reminded me often, is a mask for hurt and fear. It's what she called a "secondary emotion." Except. Except when it's not a secondary emotion. Except when it's a signal of something that deserves our attention. Except when it's signalling that we're in danger of betraying ourselves.

I don't always get it right. I'm still guilty of dismissing my anger, sometimes until it makes itself known in unhealthy ways. I recently lashed out at my son for leaving his clothes lying around the house because instead of addressing my frustration early on, I'd muttered to myself as I picked things up. My anger was telling me that I was feeling disrespected. Taken for granted. He deserved my honesty. I deserved courtesy. Instead, I got angry, he responded with anger and little got resolved.

So...I'm learning. Anger might always be a problem for me because those early-life lessons leave deep tracks in our hearts and our brains. But, slowly, I'm learning to use my anger to stand up for myself, to be certain that I'm heard.

Apologize: A Guide for Husbands

Okay guys, this one's for you:

Most of you likely didn't respond to your wife's pain around your betrayal the way renowned relationship expert Harriet Lerner suggests, which is an apology in the form of stated remorse and consistently wholehearted listening. If you're like most husbands, you said you were sorry, promised it would never happen again, it meant nothing for chrissakes, can we drop it already? And then you really *really* hoped that she would forgive you, you'd have makeup sex and then move forward into the rest of your lives. She might even be a little bit more appreciative of you now that she knew you had other options, right?

If you were a bit more realistic than that, you figured you'd go to a marriage counsellor a half-dozen times, let her cry, bow your head with genuine remorse, and even endure the insults she'd throw at you. And then, thank god, move forward into the rest of your lives.

It likely hasn't worked out like that.

But here's the thing: It hasn't worked out like we hoped it would either. Never did we imagine how excruciating betrayal was. Never did we think we'd come as unhinged as we did. We figured we'd be mad. We might execute some funny but biting revenge, like in the movies. We might meet our girlfriends and sob into a martini. But we didn't imagine there would be days we couldn't get out of bed. We didn't anticipate the confusion, the mental fog, the dull dread that took root in our stomachs or the stabbing pain in which, we swear, we could feel our hearts actually breaking.

We didn't think that, even months later, a song on the radio could reduce us to a sobbing mess on the floor. Or that a chance encounter with your affair partner could unleash in us a fury that threatened to swallow us (and you!) whole.

I've been there. So has my (still) husband. We know a thing or two about getting through this.

You? My guess is you're in uncharted waters. And so is your wife. In the interest of helping you help her through these treacherous days, weeks, months, here's your guide to apologizing for breaking her heart:

1. **Apologize.** Sounds simple, right? It's not. Do everything you can to imagine her pain. Look directly into her eyes and don't look away. See just how deep that agony goes. And then tell her how sorry you are that you weren't the husband you should have been. That she did nothing to deserve this betrayal. Repeat, as often as necessary.

2. **Be transparent.** Here's the thing about asking us to "trust me again because I've learned my lesson": Ain't gonna happen. She's sad, not stupid. You've shown her you aren't to be trusted. That's the problem with lying and cheating. It's easy to squander trust. It's really hard to earn it back. And that's what you're doing now. Earning it back. Bit by bit. By showing her, not telling her but *showing* her, that you are where you say you are, that you're with who you say you're with. I know you feel like a child. I know it's humiliating to have no privacy. Do this right and you won't live like this forever. But for now, you need to prove that you're worth taking another gamble on. And you prove that by being willing to sacrifice your privacy. If she's not worth it to you, then do yourselves a favor and leave.

3. **Work really hard to understand why you did what**

you did. Face your demons. You wouldn't have done such harm if you weren't struggling with something dark. Go to a therapist. Doesn't matter if you don't "believe" in therapy (see **Counselling, When He Doesn't Believe In**). There's a reason you risked everything that mattered to you for someone who didn't. Figure out what it is with someone who's been trained to help you. You're no good to us until you've worked out your own shame around what you've done. Until you do that, you're going to deflect, you're going to minimize, you're going to defend. None of which moves us toward healing. All of which compounds our own pain and isolation. Fix yourself first. Oh, and by the way, don't ever cheat on her again. Ever.

4. **When she tells you what she needs, give it to her.** If she wants you to read a certain book, then read it. If she wants you to call home if you're going to be late, do it. If she needs space, give it to her. If she needs closeness, give it to her. Understand that you're asking her to do the hardest thing she's ever had to do: Forgive her best friend for lying to her, for jeopardizing her physical and mental health, for subjecting her to humiliation and gossip, for betraying the promise you made to her. What is she asking you to do? Bring her flowers. Compliment her. Remind her to take a nap. Make yourself uncomfortable by talking about your issues. Doesn't seem like too much after all, does it?

5. **Help her carry the pain.** You do this by understanding it. You do this by really listening to her, over and over and over. Yes, it gets exhausting (it is for us, too). It doesn't mean you have to endure abuse, emotional or physical. It just means that, by listening to us, by answering our questions even if we've asked the same ones repeatedly (you'd be amazed at how fuzzy our brains are), you're helping us process our pain. You're shouldering a bit of the burden for us. You're showing us that our hearts can be safe with you

again. We're grateful for that, though it might be a while before we can show it.

6. **Be patient.** Healing takes a long time. Three to five years, by many experts' calculus. That doesn't mean you'll both be miserable for that long. But it does mean that there will be setbacks. There will be triggers, large and small, that elicit tears or fury, that feel as though you're back where you started. You aren't. It's a setback. And it can even be a chance for you two to remember you're on the same team, that you're working together to rebuild your marriage. Double down on the genuine remorse for creating this pain. Remind her again that you're working hard to make sure she never goes through it again. And then, for good measure, tell her that you're the luckiest guy in the world and that you're going to spend the rest of your life earning the second chance she's giving you. And that she'll never have to give you a third.

None of this is easy. But it *is* worth it. If rebuilding your marriage is what you want, I guarantee that following these steps will get you a whole lot closer to that goal. I can't guarantee that your wife will be able to move past the pain. I can't promise that she will forgive you. I have no idea whether she'll respond with a revenge affair, or file for divorce anyway, or just make your life miserable for eternity. But I do know that you will have done what you could to make reparations for the damage you caused. And I also know that, no matter what happens, you will be living your life with integrity. Which means that, whatever happens next, you're going to be a better man for it.

B

❧

Before He Cheats

Even if you're not a country music fan, you've no doubt heart this 2007 Carrie Underwood classic that has become something of a revenge anthem for betrayed wives. How many of us have fantasized about running a key along our cheating spouse's car, or brazenly taking a baseball bat to his headlights (ohhhhh, the satisfaction!) while he's in the process of hitting on some giggly girl who can't shoot whiskey?! The most surprising thing about this song isn't its success but the fact that it was written by two *guys* who managed to tap straight into the rage of betrayed women the world over.

Betrayal, How to Survive (see also Adultery)

It hurts to breathe, doesn't it? It hurts to wake up. It's impossible to fall asleep. Food makes you sick. You want nothing more than for the pain to go away. But this, you are certain, is how you will feel for the rest of your life: In excruciating pain from your husband's betrayal.

I know that feeling:

It's 2006. Just before Christmas, I finally clue in that my husband is cheating on me with his assistant at work. I confront him by phone while he's out of town on business. With her. He denies. I don't back down and, over the course of this long phone call, he admits to sex with her once, years ago.

I demand he return home immediately. A few hours later, he's at the front door.

The next few days are a blur but in between crying, screaming and giving him oral sex (see **Hysterical Bonding**), I manage to keep three young children relatively oblivious to the implosion of their parents' marriage.

Under relentless questioning by me (see also **Questions**), my husband admits more. It wasn't one night a few years ago, it was a short affair a few years ago. It wasn't just a few years ago, it was still going on until I confronted him. It had ended and then begun again. And so on. The story keeps getting worse. And more confusing.

Most of all, I'm devastated.

We see a marriage counsellor (see also **Couples Counselling**). I can't stand this counsellor's calmness. His silence when I rage. I want someone to agree with me that my husband is a monster. I don't want to work on my marriage, I want to smother my husband in his sleep. I want revenge. On him. On her. On anyone who's happy in their marriage. On anyone who ever hurt me.

I want to die. I want the pain to go away and I have no idea how to make that happen. I can't imagine a day when I won't feel this boulder of sadness on top of me.

I have my own counsellor who, literally, saves my life (see also **Antidepressants**). She lets me talk, lets me cry. Convinces me that medication might help.

It does.

Six months pass. Few people know what we've been going through except my mother and father and a couple of friends (see also **Friends, Should I Tell My**).

I've lost 15 pounds and am still on the fence about whether to stay or go. My husband has been in counselling and tells me daily how sorry he is, how desperately he wants me as his wife. I remain as confused as ever about why he cheated on me. I've spent way too much time wondering what she has that I don't, far too many hours imagining their sexual acts (see also **Mind Movies**). I swing between fury and numbness.

The numbness has allowed me to function. The fury reminds me that I'm not dead.

It's Father's Day 2007. We're in the car with our three kids, who have fallen asleep in the back seat, on our way home from a day spent with his family. My husband relays a story that seems out of character. About going to a strip bar with some guys at work a few years ago. I look at him and, in that instant, I realize I don't know the truth about his cheating. The truth about him. Not the whole truth.

I take off my wedding ring and place it on the console between us. And then I say, quietly so I don't wake our kids, "When we get home and the kids are in bed, you are going to tell me everything."

He does. And it's a bombshell. There wasn't one woman but many. It began even before he knew me and continued until I confronted him six months earlier. He is a sex addict (see also **Sex Addiction**), he tells me. He has secretly been in treatment. His counsellor had told him I would need to know. He's been preparing for this moment, even as he hoped he could avoid it.

He falls to pieces. He sobs from somewhere deep inside. He is sure it is over.

I am in shock.

I don't remember much more about that evening except this: I watch my children's father fall apart and I am scared. I tell him that I can promise him nothing but that I will remain his friend through this. My kids need a healthy, sane father.

The very next morning, we are on the phone to his counsellor. *Why?* I ask this stranger on the other end of the line. *What do these women have that I don't?*

I still remember his words and I want you to remember them too. They are the truth. "What these women have is nothing you want."

Words that began my healing.

So that's the short version of how I wound up in this club that none of us ever wants to join.

Over the next few years, we slowly rebuilt our marriage.

I created the Betrayed Wives Club, my "kickass survival site for anyone who's ever been lied to, cheated on and left for dead."

And as I wrote posts for the site, as those who visited it grew from a handful to dozens to hundreds to thousands daily, I grew too. I grew in ways that I never imagined.

You will too.

I can't promise you that your marriage will survive. I can't promise you a repentant husband who will never cheat again.

But I can promise you that you will heal from this. You will laugh again. You will feel joy.

Betrayal will become something that happened to you, not the whole of your life. I promise.

Bobbitt, Lorena

In 1993, Lorena Bobbitt cut off her husband's penis with a kitchen knife, thereby becoming something of a folk hero for betrayed wives everywhere, and making her husband the punchline of jokes for eternity. However, it wasn't just her husband's infidelities (and his flaunting of those) that led her to penile dismemberment but years of emotional, physical, and sexual abuse. Indeed, it was following a rape by her husband that she took action. Lorena Bobbitt was found not guilty by reason of insanity. Her lawyers successfully argued that the PTSD she experienced from years of abuse caused an "irresistible impulse" to cut off her husband's penis. Yes, I know many of us have felt this impulse. Resist.

Books, Healing from Betrayal

About a week after discovering my husband's infidelity, I drove to a bookstore and began looking for books that might help me understand what had happened in my marriage and how I might survive it. In essence, I was looking for a book like the one you're either holding in your hands or reading on your device. I wanted a survival guide, a blueprint, a map, all rolled into one. I couldn't find one. I did, however, find a memoir titled "Back From Betrayal." I recognized her pain, which validated my own. I devoured it in two days. Books are how I make sense of the world so it's no surprise that I've turned to many to help me through this. And so have many others on the Betrayed Wives Club who recommend these titles:

"When Things Fall Apart" by Pema Chodron

"Private Lies" by Frank Pittman

"Not Just Friends" by Shirley Glass

"How Can I Forgive You?" and "After the Affair" by Janis A. Spring

Any of the "Dance of..." books by Harriet Lerner

"Too Good to Leave, Too Bad to Stay" by Mira Kirshenbaum

"Getting Past the Affair" by Douglas Snyder

"The Monogamy Myth" by Peggy Vaughan

"Intimate Treason" by Claudia Black

"When Your Love is a Liar" by Susan Forward

"Your Sexually Addicted Spouse" by Marsha Means and Barbara Steffans

"Our Cheating Hearts" by Kate Figes

"Love You, Hate the Porn" by Mark Chamberlain

"The Body Keeps the Score" by Bessel Van Der Kolk

"Forgive and Forget, Healing the Hurts You Didn't Deserve" by Lewis Smedes

Any books by Brené Brown, especially "The Gifts of Imperfection" and "Rising Strong"

"Mending a Shattered Heart: A Guide for Partners of Sex Addicts" by Stefanie Carnes

Boundaries

Boundaries are what we put in place to keep ourselves safe. We learn them in childhood, like telling that bossy kid in kindergarten to get her hands off your paintbrush because you were creating a masterpiece. And then our families or our friends or our husbands, bolstered by our culture, convince us that boundaries are selfish or self-centered, that our bodies and our hearts exist to deliver what others want.

If there's anything that will bring our boundaries (or lack of) into sharp focus, it's being betrayed.

Pre-betrayal, my boundaries, if I'd known enough to pay attention to them, were telling me in a hundred different ways that my marriage felt unfair. My anger and resentment were clear cues that my feelings and my actions did not match up. What did I do? I tried to talk myself out of my feelings: I was probably expecting too much. Why couldn't I ever just be happy? After all, he was better than a lot of husbands I knew.

Big mistake. By ignoring my own boundaries, I was disrespecting myself, which gave everyone else permission to do the same.

But when my husband cheated on me and then begged me to try to rebuild our marriage, I realized that the old marriage was not an option for me. If I was going to stay and work through this shitstorm that he'd created, I was going to darn well get something good out of it. Not just him but a new improved him and a new improved me and a new improved marriage in which I was not doing everything for everyone and hiding behind a bitter smile.

So...boundaries.

I hadn't a clue what they were and why I needed them. I had considered myself something of a badass independent woman. I ran marathons. I ran my own business. I had friends, men and women, of my own. I travelled solo all over the world. Plus...I was nice. Nice is good, right?

Turns out, not so much. Nice is good when you have clear boundaries and the ability to state your needs unequivocally. Nice is good when it doesn't stop you from being not-nice when your boundaries are getting trampled on.

For me, nice was a way of paying for others' positive attention with my self-worth.

The baby's crying at 3 a.m. and I'm exhausted. Oh, well, honey, you sleep. I'm awake anyway.

You need to work late again and I'm on deadline? That's okay. I'll just work when the kids are asleep.

This wasn't about compromise. This was about me playing the martyr. This was about acquiescence and total disrespect for myself. I was so invested in being a good sport, in being that great supportive wife who never really asks for anything because, well, whatever you want to give me is probably swell.

As therapist, author and podcaster Esther Perel puts it, "When did you start settling for crumbs?"

Being nice (which is a "nice" way of saying "pleasing people") often gets in the way of having and enforcing boundaries.

Post betrayal? Screw nice. I want to be heard. And respected. And so...boundaries.

(What's especially interesting for me is that I'm able to be far nicer now that I respect my own boundaries. It's impossible to be genuinely nice when resentment is seeping out of your pores. Your words might sound "nice" but your actions will be passive-aggressive.)

So, let's outline what boundaries are...and are not. Boundaries are your rules for your life. Shame researcher and author Brené Brown says boundaries are an act of compassion for yourself.

They're about respecting what you need to be your best self. To feel safe. To feel valued. To feel heard.

Boundaries are not about controlling others. It's not a boundary to say, "I think eating meat is cruel so everybody around me must eat vegetarian." It is a boundary to say "I think eating meat is cruel so when I prepare a meal, I will only prepare vegetarian." In the first, you're trying to control others' actions. In the second, you're controlling only your own.

But boundaries in the wake of betrayal get a bit blurry because we're asking our partners to respect what we need and it might look a lot different than what we need in a healthy relationship that hasn't been marked by infidelity. A healthy post-betrayal boundary is: Your dishonesty has made me feel unsafe in this relationship. I need to know that you are where you say you are and you are with whom you say you are in order to begin rebuilding trust, which is why I will be checking your phone or installing a GPS locator on it.

In a faithful relationship, I think monitoring each others' whereabouts is controlling and creepy. Post-betrayal, however, it's a way to rebuild trust. As time goes on, the vigilance should decrease. Again, it's about respecting your need for safety and assurance, not controlling your partner.

But this aspect of control can become problematic. And I hear often from betrayed wives about partners who've cheated becoming angry at being "controlled" by these post-betrayal boundaries. I get it. It must suck to be monitored. It must feel humiliating to have to come home right after work instead of stopping for a beer with friends. But the way I see it, a partner who's cheated has a lot of trust to rebuild. This isn't about paying penance, it's about supporting a loyal wife who has been deeply hurt and whose boundaries take priority right now. Not always...but right now. Compromise and negotiation can come later. Right now, it's about your emotional safety.

Here's the thing: Those of us who've been betrayed get to set the rules for reconciliation. As one of our betrayed soul-warriors on the site put it, "My heartbreak, my rules." (See also, **My Heartbreak, My Rules.**) That's boundaries. But while we're still getting our feet wet regarding boundaries, many of us aren't so likely to enforce those rules. So it's important to establish boundaries early on that set us up for success, not failure.

What I mean by this is, establish boundaries that empower you. And give a lot of careful thought to what the consequences are if those boundaries are violated.

Again, boundaries aren't about controlling him, they're about taking care of yourself and establishing emotional safety. If he won't support you in your healing, then find support anywhere else you can. Therapy. Websites. Books. Trusted friends.

No matter how anyone else in the world responds to your suffering right now, you can respect your own feelings. You can tell yourself that you matter. You can orchestrate your healing.

If he wants to join you and support you, that's wonderful. He can start by respecting your boundaries.

But – and this is important – if he's refusing or reluctant to support you in your healing, then perhaps he's telling you loud and clear that you don't matter as much as you should. You can't make someone respect you. But you can show him what respect and compassion look like by giving it to yourself.

C

Cake-eater, How to Spot A

If you've visited any of the online infidelity sites, you're aware that there's a whole new language to learn (see also **Lexicon for Betrayed Wives**). Cake-eater is, of course, a reference to the old proverb, "you can't have your cake and eat it too." In other words, if you eat your cake, it's gone. In other *other* words, you can't have it both ways. A cake-eater is a guy who likes the security of marriage but wants the high of an affair. A cake-eater is not someone who's likely to make himself over into Husband of the Year. Cake-eaters are often unconcerned with the pain they've caused and are, instead, eager to keep eating cake and having it too. They wallow in self-pity because of the situation they're in ("I have to choose? Oh, the *unfairness* of it all!"). They do just enough to make you think they're choosing you – counselling, promises of No Contact, passionate sex. But when pressed, they Just. Can't. Totally. Commit. My advice? To paraphrase Marie Antoinette, let him eat cake. He just can't be married to you at the same time. (A fence-sitter is a close relative.)

Carnes, Patrick

Sometimes called the pioneer of sex addiction research, Patrick Carnes coined the term 'sex addiction' and created a treatment center focussed on helping those for whom sexual behaviour had become an addiction. He's also the author of a whole lot of books about sex addiction, including "Don't Call It Love: Recovery from Sexual Addiction" and "Out of the Shadows: Understanding Sexual Addiction."

His books are compassionate and comprehensive and I found them indispensable in helping me understand my husband's behaviour. At no point does Carnes give sex addicts a pass for their behaviour. Rather they are held accountable and expected to adhere to a stringent program, modelled on Alcoholics Anonymous' 12-steps.

Cheater

My husband objected any time I called him a "cheater." He could tolerate "jerk," even "asshole." But "cheater" seemed to cross a line into something that he couldn't stand to categorize himself as. It was his Kryptonite. And so I used it whenever I wanted to emotionally hobble him, which was fairly often in those early pain-filled days. I was not exactly at my most Dalai Lama-esque. But, c'mon: Cheater. One who cheats.

Child of the Affair

Phoenix, a brave and compassionate member of our secret sisterhood, wrote this about living with her ex's child of the affair:

It's betrayal on a whole new level.

There was a feeling that something else really sacred had been violated. Sharing pregnancy and childbirth, the miracle and the beauty, was a special bond we shared. When he shared it with her, it no longer felt special. They ruined that for me, like they ruined so many other things. When I remember the births of my children, there is a sadness and a taint there now. I'm hoping it fades with time.

As mother of his child, the Other Woman gets a status and respect she doesn't deserve and hasn't earned.

There are more triggers. For a year, looking at babies or hearing the words "little brother" made me unhappy. Which sucks, because I love babies. That is getting a little better.

I am now permanently chained to her and to the most traumatic event of my life. It will always have a presence in my life because my children are related to her child. That won't go away. Ever. The injustice of that was devastating.

I am often conflicted because every child is precious. But what this child represents to me is horrible. I would never hold it against him, it is not his fault. But I can't completely separate him from it in my mind. Maybe one day.

The situation with my children is excruciating. I have to watch their joy and delight in a little brother, which they've always wanted, while grappling with the fact that they have a brother who is not related to me. One of the most significant events in their lives – and not only am I excluded from it, but the very thought of it makes me bitter and sad. The best me I know is the me that can celebrate with my girls because their little brother took his first steps, and they got to see it. But that is the surface me. The hidden me is flinching from yet another blow. The blows keep coming. They won't stop.

I have felt powerless. There was nothing I could do to stop two selfish people from changing my family forever.

And my children are not just tied to that precious, innocent boy. Through him, they are tied to HER. A heartless skank who still pretends that I do not exist because it would be inconvenient to her view of the world. She is part of their family.

These are all thoughts I've had over the last year and a half. They are not all present every day, all the time.

These are the wounds that have to be processed, accepted, and healed.

Learning to accept THIS kind of change in your life takes another level of strength and endurance.

But never did I consider keeping the children apart, or keeping his existence from them. I could never do that to my girls. And if something happened to my ex, I would hold my nose and deal with the OW so that my kids could see their brother. The children, all the children, are innocent.

I'm hoping that one day the pain will fade to the point that I can be a small part of his life, as the mother of his sisters...someone who cares about his welfare and is kind to him. Someone whose life was once changed in a very painful way by his birth, but that was so long ago that nobody thinks about it anymore.

That's the dream, but even though I've met him once, touched his little hands and looked into innocent eyes that reminded me of my older daughter's, even so, I have a long way to go.

Children, Should You Tell Your

This is something that you may not have control over. If, for instance, your child is the one that stumbles onto nude pics on dad's phone of a woman who is decidedly not mom. But children, though they're part of a family, are not part of a marriage. What happens between the married people in the family needs to stay between the married people. Even in the case of divorce or separation, children should not have to know the gruesome details no matter how satisfying it might feel to out your husband as the cheating scumbag that he is and gather allies. Remember Michelle Obama telling us "When they go low, we go high"? This situation is tailor-made for that sentiment. Protect your children as much as possible.

That said, children have radar for any potential threats to their survival. And the H-Bomb that is infidelity is definitely a threat to their survival. Validate their concerns. My children were between the ages of three and eight when I learned of my husband's cheating. Suddenly their mom was behind closed doors, crying. Or a vacant-eyed zombie. They were scared. And so I told them that "mommy and daddy were having problems" but that we were seeking help. My eldest asked if we were getting a divorce. I told her that we were working hard to not get divorced but admitted that "marriage is really hard." And I reassured them often that they were loved and safe. In short, I responded to my kids in a way that I wished my parents had responded to me when I was nine years old and answered the phone from a man insisting that my father was cheating with his wife.

Lynn Less Pain, one of our BWC members who grew up in a home where an affair had gone on for seven years, also had a different approach with older children:

Be honest, according to their age. I insisted my pigskin man in tuna town call each one of his children and apologize. If you remain silent then your kids can come up with all this other shit in their head, never tell you because they want to protect mom and take several years to fester into a person that you don't know, is uncontrollable and needs serious therapy. Protect your children always no matter what. Let them see you angry but not crazy. Let them see you cry but know it is not their fault.

Circle of Trust

I had a (tiny) handful of people I trusted to tell what was going on. They included my mother, two friends and a therapist. These people were my lifeline. That's what you're looking for. No drama. No judgement. No gossip.

An online community (such as Betrayed Wives Club) can be a huge source of support among people who understand what you're going through. And – bonus! – you can hide behind a pseudonym.

Cloud Appreciation Society

One of my favorite books is called "The Cloud Collector's Handbook" by a guy named Gavin Pretor-Pinney, who founded the Cloud Appreciation Society (www.cloudappreciationsociety.org). He thinks our culture suffers from "blue sky thinking," this notion that everything should always be good and free of obstacles. He urges us to contemplate the clouds as more than just something that gets in the way of the sun. Clouds have their own beauty, he says, and "exist in a constant state of flux, shifting effortlessly from one form to another.... They're like expressions in the face of the sky."

Clouds remind me that nothing stays the same forever. What looks like storm clouds "arcus" today will give way to wispy white "cumulus fractus" tomorrow.

Codependency

I first came across this word in my 20s, reading books about growing up in an alcoholic family. A codependent, I read, is someone who supports or enables an addict's behaviour. Examples included a wife who called in sick for her alcoholic husband when he was hungover, or a child who lied to protect an addict parent. Mostly, my codependency showed up by overlooking or excusing behaviour that was immature, unkind, or unhealthy. A whole lot of therapy helped and, by the time I got married in my early 30s, I thought I had beaten codependency.

And then came D-Day.

And then came D-Day 2.

And with D-Day 2, came the insistence by a whole lot of experts in sex addiction that the partner of an addict is codependent.

I'm not buying it.

For one thing, there is absolutely no way that I supported or enabled my husband's acting out. I had no idea he was acting out. Absolutely not a clue. And if I had known, I can promise you that I would not have tolerated it for a second.

But, and it's a big but, despite my initial refusal to acknowledge any codependency on my part, I can see now that I did allow my husband to disengage from our family. I accepted his routine "working late" excuses. I overlooked how late he stayed up on the computer. I rolled my eyes at his inappropriate sexual "jokes." None of which makes me complicit in his behaviour. But, in hindsight, there were signs that all was not well.

All of which is to say, codependency is something that many of us who grew up in dysfunctional homes learned well. And it can be really tough to completely unlearn. Too often we tolerate behaviour that others, with the benefit of healthier boundaries, would not. Even if we don't know the full extent of those behaviours.

Counselling, When He Doesn't Believe In

Let's start with this: Therapy isn't something one "believes" in, like Bigfoot or fairies or alien abductions. So when someone says they don't "believe" in therapy, what he's really saying is he doesn't believe that talking with an objective professional about his life and his problems is going to help him.

To which I say, "How is not talking about your problems working out for you?" Yeah. That's what I thought.

Therapy is, of course, a broad term for a whole lot of approaches to helping people move through problems that are getting in the way of leading a productive, healthy life. Not "believing" in therapy is a cop out. Far more truthful to say, "I don't want to go."

To admit that he doesn't want to go, however, opens your husband up to your disappointment or your anger and frustration. He'd prefer to hide behind the fiction that therapy won't work for him, so why not save time and money by not bothering with it at all. After all, he'll tell you, it's bogus. Or he doesn't like to talk. He'll refer to therapy as woo-woo head-shrinking stuff for crazy people. Surely not for someone as sane and feet-on-the-ground as a guy like him whose only problem is that he violated his marriage vows, lied to his partner and risked losing a marriage that he now claims he never wanted to lose.

That avoidance of discomfort is exactly the kind of behaviour that got him into this situation. By not being forthright and honest, he created this shitstorm that he now wishes would just go away without him having to do anything that he doesn't want to do. Or rather, that he doesn't "believe" in.

I came to therapy reluctantly. I grew up in a home with addiction, depression, anxiety, suicide attempts and strife. When my mother got sober and sane, I was 20 and launching into my life. My mom suggested therapy because she, correctly, saw that I held a lot of anger about my earlier years. I refused, insisting that I was "fine" and that I didn't need some stranger telling me how to feel.

A few years later, however, as I struggled within a highly toxic relationship with a man I couldn't imagine living without, I relented.

I thought a therapist could help me figure out how to make this guy love me enough to stay. Instead, she helped me find the self-respect and strength to leave.

Which could be a big piece of why your husband doesn't "believe" in therapy. There's huge fear for many people in discovering just what's lurking in their own hearts, and that of their partners. For those people, pretending that everything is fine is preferable to knowing it isn't. They might even have convinced themselves that, all evidence aside, everything *is* fine. If only you could just stop talking about their mistakes, about the destruction they've caused. After all, they won't do it again.

Until they do. Or are, at least, tempted.

All of us lack certain tools in our emotional toolbox. I don't know a single person whose parents were able to provide them exactly the number and type of tools they would need to handle whatever life throws their way. Some of us can develop our own healthy tools, but far more of us rely on crappy, rusty tools to cope – we drink, we shop, we ignore, we rage, we cheat – or we fall apart completely.

Somewhere in there, the smart ones among us say one thing: "Help."

We realize that if we were so awesome at solving our own problems, we wouldn't be in this mess. We acknowledge that our way of coping has created some highly unpleasant side-effects, like a wife whose eyes hold a world of pain that we caused.

And then, the wise and courageous ones allow themselves to consider that maybe, just maybe, this therapy thing is worth a try.

It might not work with the first therapist. It might require a few tries. But my guess is that these same guys would continue to find a good mechanic for their car if the first one didn't seem too great rather than decide that they don't "believe" in mechanics.

It will undoubtedly require a lot of ego-checking and patience as everyone finds their footing and begins to establish an atmosphere of trust. After all, you should all be there for the same reason: to create a healthy relationship based on honesty, respect, compassion and clear boundaries.

Because that, whether or not these guys will admit it, is what everyone is after. And, too bad for them, part of that process is going to require that this guy who doesn't "believe" in therapists, has to dig deep into his psyche and figure out why he risked losing what mattered for something that didn't. Or at least didn't matter as much.

He should want this. He should be willing to do whatever it takes to begin to heal this damage he created. He should be willing to make himself uncomfortable in order to help you feel safe again.

If he won't? If he continues to hide behind this baloney that therapy requires belief rather than hard work, then he's telling you that this marriage isn't worth the effort required to heal it.

This is painful but crucial information for you to have. It makes your choice – whether to stay in the marriage with full awareness of how much effort he's willing to put into rebuilding it, or whether to leave with that same awareness – a lot more clear.

I'm not insisting that no marriage can be saved without therapy. I am saying that I don't know of any. Sure, I know of marriages that survived infidelity without therapy. But I don't know of solid, happy marriages that have. The solid, happy marriages I know of that have survived infidelity have done so with a team of support, from friends to, yes, therapists. Personal therapists, marriage therapists, family therapists. Cognitive behavioural therapy, EMDR, couples counselling.

So while it's possible that a marriage can be rebuilt without the help of counsellors to guide couples toward healing, I don't believe it's helpful to anyone to ignore the valuable assistance of an objective, experienced therapist.

BWC member Lynn Less Pain says this:

Don't let him blow you off. Do not accept that your husband knows what is best for your marriage, what YOU need or don't need, in this process. Don't allow him to put his own shame and hurt, because of his actions, ahead of what you need. He did that during the affair...

Countermoves

Countermoves are almost inevitable whenever we make our boundaries clear.

Countermoves are the reactions we get from people who far prefer our boundaries to be fuzzy and easily manipulated.

We see them transparently with kids. Think of the last time you told a child he/she couldn't do something – watch TV, have a cookie before dinner, stay up late. Did the child respond with, "I understand. And I appreciate you even considering my request."

Didn't think so.

More likely you heard something like "You're the meanest person in the world. Jeremy's mother lets him [fill-in-the-blank-here] anytime he wants. I hate you." Or maybe you heard: "You're not the boss of me. I can do whatever I want." Or perhaps it was something like: "Fine. I don't care. I didn't want that anyway." There's usually some eye-rolling, or arm-crossing, or stomping involved. Frequently there's sulking.

Depending on our own personalities and understanding of boundaries and countermoves, we're likely to get hooked into one type of countermove more than others. For me, it's anger.

The minute someone in my family gets angry at me, I'm hooked and I'll match them holler for holler.

Countermoves by the adults in our lives aren't always so transparent.

Do any of these sound familiar?

"You're just like your mother."

"You only think of yourself."

"You're so controlling."

"You're acting crazy."

"Your father is very upset that you didn't [fill-in-the-blank]."

"Stop being jealous."

"Nothing makes you happy."

Maybe the countermoves aren't words but actions. Storming out of a room. Slamming a door. Banging a fist on a table. The silent treatment.

Whether words or actions, countermoves are about getting us to back down. And they often work. The last thing we want is to sound like our mother. Or act selfish. Or controlling. Or crazy. And so we insist that we're not doing that at all...are we? And in that instant, our boundaries get fuzzy. We soften things a bit. "It's just that I can't sleep until I know you're home..." or "I just need to know that you're not in touch with her...." Those "just"s or "I only..."s weaken our boundaries.

Barbara Coloroso, who's a parenting expert but whose advice works with anyone in our lives, calls these typical countermoves "cons":

Con 1 is weeping, wailing, begging, bribing, gnashing of teeth. ("Please stop reading my texts. It's humiliating. You're treating me like a child. I'm fed up.")

Con 2 is anger and aggression. ("How dare you check my phone! You violated my privacy. If you won't trust me then there's no point in staying married.")

Con 3 is sulking/pouting. ("Fine. Check my bloody phone whenever you want. You're not going to find anything...")

Cons are powerful. They hook us and if we're not good boundary-enforcers, next thing we know, we've backed down.

But when we back down, we poison the relationship with our own negative feelings. Resentment. Frustration. Anger. Hurt. Fear.

We might have kept the peace for the moment, but we've paid for it by contributing to the dysfunction.

What does this look like after betrayal? Well, let's continue with the example above – to have total transparency around your partner's phone or computer. In the short-term, we want passwords and access to all records and accounts.

It would be lovely if our partner responds that he understands that this is part of rebuilding trust. Many, however, give us countermoves.

"You're never going to trust me again, are you? No matter what I do, you find fault with it. I can't win with you."

Or: "I refuse to live like a prisoner in my own home. I told you I wouldn't cheat again. I've learned my lesson. If you can't believe me, that's your problem."

Or: "You need to just trust me. Let's put this in the past and move forward. It's unhealthy to keep talking about it."

What's more, some of it is probably true. You likely are hard to please right now (uh, duh. Wonder why?). You are also doubting you'll ever trust him again. But that doesn't make the countermoves less toxic. And it doesn't change the fact that you are making a reasonable request under the circumstances. You're drawing clear boundaries in order to respect yourself within the relationship.

You can commiserate if you'd like: "I'm sure it does seem humiliating to have to show me your phone messages but I need to see them in order to silence my fears that you're still cheating on me." You can murmur sympathetically that, "Yes, it does seem as though I'm hard to please right now." But that doesn't change the fact that you're respecting yourself and what you need within the relationship.

Recognizing and responding to countermoves gets easier with practice.

At a certain point, when we consistently refuse to back down, the people in our lives realize that the countermoves aren't going to work.

And they either stop...or find others with whom the unhealthy dance can continue.

Either way, we win.

Couples Counsellor, How to Find a Good

We're messy people. All of us, not just those of us dealing with infidelity. We're the product of our parents, our culture, our personality, our education, our friends. And inevitably there are some experiences in there that mess with us, whether a bit or a whole lot. Which means that there isn't a soul among us who can't benefit from the occasional tune-up – the chance to examine the thoughts and values we hold and determine how they're contributing to our psychological health and our actions. However – and this is a big however – therapy is only as good as the person offering it. A bad therapist – and I've heard some stories of really bad therapists – can do serious damage. I know of a woman who sought therapy with her husband to help their marriage survive the incredible changes after the wife suffered a spinal stroke, rendering her paralyzed. The husband and the therapist began a relationship right under the wife's nose. I know, right?

I often get asked how to know if a therapist is good. Well, in the case above, it's pretty obvious, though only after the fact. The couples therapist of one betrayed wife had suggested the Other Woman join the therapy to clear the air. This, in case it needs stating, is nuts.

Put simply, a good therapist is one who helps each partner in the marriage become better able to hear and respond to the other. My husband and I knew just how good our own therapist was when we realized that she had created an environment where there was no good guy or bad guy, though she acknowledged that one of us (me!) was coming into therapy with a wound caused by the other's (his!) dumbass choice to cheat.

Don't be afraid to walk away from a therapist who's making you uncomfortable. Sometimes it's just too soon for therapy and you need time to catch your breath. Ask yourself if the discomfort comes from feeling re-victimized or if the therapist is urging you to examine things you'd prefer to leave unexamined. In other words, is the discomfort shouting at you to back away (unsafe) or whispering to you to move closer (scary). Unsafe is your cue to remove yourself from the situation. Scary is your clue that there are some things you've been avoiding.

I hear from a lot of betrayed wives whose husbands refuse therapy, insisting that they can solve their own problems. That's a red flag for me. If one of the partners feels the need to get marital counselling, I'm a firm believer that the other owes them to at least try it. Those who refuse therapy, in my experience, are the ones who need it most. They've spent a lifetime avoiding a deeper look at their own pain.

But I'm no expert. So I took your questions to Valerie, a couples therapist who often helps those coping with infidelity.

Elle: Betrayed women often write to me noting that a therapist has insisted they take "responsibility" for the state of the marriage, which feels to them as if they're being blamed for their spouse's affair. What do you think about that?

Therapist: The therapists in question have abandoned a neutral-compassionate stance in favor of a moral perspective. This is in fact "victim blaming." In an age of Dr. Phil and the reign of social conservatism, people believe they need to find a therapist who will tell them they did wrong or defend them if they have been wronged. The therapist as judge and jury. That isn't good therapy.

E: What about a betrayed wife's need to see her spouse accept responsibility for the pain he's caused by his infidelity?

T: The therapist's role is not to force accountability on either part. Accountability will evolve naturally in the course of therapy that is encouraging of empathy and compassion on both parts. For example, the betrayed partner cannot and will not move past hurt unless he or she feels that her partner demonstrates real empathy for the harm done. Similarly, the affair partner will not come out of the shadows and into the light (so to speak) unless he or she feels their partner can grasp what lies beyond the betrayal. We are not talking causality here – that is the proverbial chicken and egg question – but rather a relational dance that a good therapist will be attuned to and work with.

E: Should all couples dealing with infidelity seek therapy?

T: Some couples will not be helped by therapy. It is a gruelling process, and each party must be prepared to go in with a view to self-reflection. If the hurt is still very raw, or too much damage has been done, the participation will only be about deflecting, blaming, punishing, hiding, etc. A good therapist will tell a couple they aren't ready and that individual work around stabilizing and returning to self should be undertaken first. A good therapist will always help the couple set limits around damaging behaviours before proceeding, a process which involves both parties agreeing to work toward change.

E: So what should people coping with the aftermath of infidelity be looking for?

T: Find a therapist who is relationally oriented with an understanding of family systems theory. The therapist should show compassion and understanding for both partners right from the initial session. Not an easy task. If the therapist is preaching or wagging a finger in either direction, I would say run away!

D

D-Day

We betrayed wives talk a lot about D-Day. Historically, of course, D-Day was the beginning of the end of the Second World War, when the allied forces invaded Normandy and caught Germany by surprise. In the world of infidelity, however, D-Day refers to "Discovery Day" or "Disclosure Day," the date *we* were caught by surprise. It marks the metaphorical end of our current marriage.

It is a day that lives, at least in our minds, in infamy. And it is hell. There are things we can do, however, that amount to triage for our battered soul.

First, reduce expectations of yourself to zero. (Though aim to keep yourself out of jail.)

My expectations during that horrible time were ridiculous. I not only expected myself to know how to respond to this unprecedented marital crisis, I expected myself to be able to function the same as I had the day before the bomb hit. To prepare dinner, to help children with homework, to meet my work deadlines.

Reduce expectations to zero. Immediate triage for your soul. Focus on three things only:

1. Eat enough food that you don't die. More, if possible.

2. Sleep, even if it requires the help of sleep-aids, such as melatonin, an antihistamine (occasional use only), or something your doctor prescribed to help you. (Avoid alcohol or illegal drugs. The idea isn't to make things worse.)

3. Breathe. In and out. In and out. Deeply if you can. If the idea of breathing is more than you can bear, please reach out for help. Google the suicide helpline for your country. Call a trusted friend. Or your doctor. I promise you the pain will end. But you have to be around for that to happen.

Here's what you should not focus on right now. Remember, reduce expectations to zero.

•Will my marriage survive? Who knows. Not you right now, so don't expect to know. Give yourself time to absorb the shock. Clarity will come with time.

•Is he lying to me? Probably. You likely don't have all the information right now. But that's okay. You'll come to realize there are things you don't need to know. What you do know – that he cheated on you – is enough right now.

•Will my life ever be the same? Nope. But that's not the same as saying it won't be great. I promise you will get through this. You will not feel this pain forever. You will laugh again. You will feel joy again. I don't know what your life will look like and neither do you. Even if he hadn't cheated, none of us knows what the future holds. We never did.

Eat, sleep, breathe.

There will, undoubtedly, be other demands. You might have children that require parenting. You might have work that requires doing. There are some things we can't avoid. Just getting out of bed is a Herculean feat, so give yourself huge props for doing so.

The day will come for figuring things out. The day will come for choices. The day will come for achievement. But right now, the day has come for self-compassion and self-care, for triage of your soul.

Dear Sugar

A bride wrote a letter to Dear Sugar, the advice column on The Rumpus website, about how to cope with the news that her brother-in-law, who she adored, had cheated on her sister. Bride wanted this couple to walk her down the aisle. Now, with news that this marriage she admired had been marked by infidelity, Bride wasn't so sure.

The response offered by Dear Sugar was pitch-perfect and it includes this:

[Your sister] was actually trying to tell you the secret. In allowing you a more intimate view of her much-touted but flawed marriage, your sister was attempting to show you what a real perfect couple looks like: happy, humane, and occasionally all fucked up. I can't imagine anyone more fitting to walk you down the aisle on your wedding day than your sister and her husband, two people who've kept their love and friendship alive for more than twenty-five years. That you're doubting this after learning not all of those years were easy, tells me there's something deeper at work here that has nothing to do with their marriage and everything to do with your own insecurities and fears.

Depression

Depression's biggest lie is that life isn't worth living.

I believed that. I believed it so much that I thought about ways to kill myself. After swimming my entire childhood in a murky soup of emotional neglect and shame, I thought I'd built my adult life on solid ground. So when that turned out to be an illusion, I wanted to give up. I told my therapist I was too tired. Too tired of getting knocked down and picking myself up. Too tired of being hurt. Too tired to convince myself that life wasn't just a slog to the end.

She urged me to try antidepressants. I resisted them.

But, given that the only other viable alternative for me seemed to be swerving my bike into the path of an oncoming truck (I figured it would be considered an accident and my kids would not suffer the stigma of a mother who killed herself, as my own had attempted more than once), I agreed to try the meds.

Within a few days, the clouds seemed to lift slightly. Within a couple of weeks, I had the energy to put some effort into getting dressed.

And slowly, with therapy and time and those detested meds, the depression lifted. I also revisited those old childhood wounds, ripped open from my husband's betrayal, and challenged many of my deeply entrenched beliefs: that I never quite measured up no matter how perfect my life appeared on the outside; that people only cared about me because they didn't know the 'real' me. I can see now that I vastly overestimated my ability to fool people and vastly underestimated the love and compassion that exists in this world. Turns out, this imperfect me is perfectly lovable.

But though my experience with depression was easily treated, I know how debilitating depression can sometimes be. Depression sucks the marrow from our bones. It turns us into shadows.

The you – that beautiful, divine you that the world needs – is still there. And you need to fight like hell to find your way into the sunlight again. Maybe it's with the help of meds. Maybe it's with the help of a therapist or two or three. It takes a village, after all. Maybe it's with the support of a remorseful spouse or with the absence of one who never deserved you in the first place.

Depression is real, it's horrible and it can absolutely be brought on by the deep wound of betrayal.

But don't let it be fatal.

Divorce/Separation

StillStanding1, frequent wise contributor to Betrayed Wives Club, has this to say about separation and divorce:

A separation is scary. It may be one of the hardest, bravest things you will ever do. It may or may not be the thing that saves your marriage, but if you put the work in, I'm pretty sure it will save you.

I'm not advocating separation for everyone post D-Day. If you have a remorseful spouse who is doing the work, it's reasonable to remain together and work this through. Being together gives you opportunities to reconnect and communicate. There are, however, situations where a separation might give you the time and space to breathe and think about what the next right thing is for you.

•When your spouse continues to blatantly continue the affair. This is incredibly harmful to you. You are already traumatized and in PTSD high alert.

•When your spouse, after attempting reconciliation, resumes contact and doesn't disclose this to you or resumes the full affair. More pain and trauma for you.

•When your spouse violates any of your rules for reconciliation: refuses counselling, refuses transparency, refuses to disclose contact, continues inappropriate friendships, lies about where they are or what they are doing. Whatever your requirements are. I'm not talking about a mistake or momentary lapse. I'm talking about willful, ongoing, intentional violations of your terms.

•When your spouse is gaslighting you (see also ***Gaslighting****), manipulating you or children (if you have them), starting fights and arguments and then shifting blame onto you. Do you feel like every-*

thing is always your fault? Do you come out of conversations wondering what the hell just happened? You may be experiencing gaslighting.

•When you are a long way out from D-Day, but your spouse has not done the work and is more interested in sweeping things under the rug than dealing with your pain.

A managed separation may give you relief from the immediate pain so that you can sort out the larger issues. It may also be the wake-up call for your wayward spouse. Enough is enough, you say. Here's a dose of what life will be like without me. Sometimes this works. Sometimes it doesn't. Taking care of yourself and getting you out of harm's way is the primary motivation behind choosing a separation.

There are many different types of separations that can range from in-house, psychological separations to physical, pre-divorce separations. If you and your spouse are trying to work things out but are stuck, an in-house separation might give you room to breathe and send a clear message that he needs to step up. If your spouse is still fully engaged in destructive behaviours, getting him out from under your roof so he can't cause new, daily pain, might be the option you need. Consider seeing a marriage or family counsellor together to help guide you through a separation process, especially if children are involved and you will be physically separating.

Deciding to separate was scary. It was six abusive, ambivalent, roller-coaster months post D-Day before I finally told him he needed to move out. And even then, he manipulated me into it because he was too much of a coward to just leave and own what he was doing. We continued to meet with the marriage counsellor and she became our separation manager. She helped us outline how we'd manage communication, the kids, schedules and the type of separation we would be doing. It was to be a constructive separation – in which we each took physical time apart to find ourselves, work on our own issues and break old patterns of communications and behaviour so we could potentially come back together in a healthy way. He moved out three months after I told him he needed to leave. This was the time frame we planned with the counsellor and allowed him time to find a place and for us to plan together how we were going to present this to our kids.

You can decide if you still go to counselling during the separation, with the purpose of working on your relationship or, less often, with the purpose of managing any conflict or housekeeping items. We continued for four months until he announced that he wanted a divorce (this is another story and includes some of the classics of Stupid Sh!t Cheaters Say.) We started working with a mediator toward divorce.

During the separation, I took the counsellor's advice to dig into my stuff. If you are working on this on your own, turn your focus from the relationship on to you. This will have enormous pay-offs whether you remain together or eventually part.

E

❦

Eat, What to (See "Infidelity Diet")

My friend Angie vomited a few times a day and couldn't keep food down. Ally couldn't get anything past the lump in her throat. Everything tasted like sawdust in my mouth. Within a few weeks, I'd lost 10 pounds. A month later, I was down another five. It's called the Infidelity Diet because so many of us, after discovering our partner's cheating, lose weight. And though it was nice to slip easily into my skinny jeans, it's hardly healthy to lose weight so fast. Especially when we need our strength.

I crowdsourced the Club to see what they ate to keep themselves alive:

Smoothies: If you have a blender, then throw in fruit, spinach, yogurt, hemp or flax seed, protein powder. Do not add tequila. Blend and sip.

Soup: If you can't or don't want to make your own, find a nearby market. Added bonus is the comfort that soup can offer.

Toast: Easy. Cheap. Top with peanut butter or jam or the entrails of your husband.

Cereal: "I lived on cereal," says one Betrayed Wife, who notes it took zero effort to make or clean up.

Fruit: Keep a bowl handy. If you peel an orange, you might as well eat the whole thing. A bunch of grapes (next best thing to wine!) can offer some nutrients. Slice an apple or a banana. "I ate a lot of apples as part of getting in the moment," says StillStanding1. "I would focus on the apple. The texture, the tart, sweetness, the flavor and the little boost of energy I got because I was otherwise starving."

Meal replacement drinks: Ensure. Boost. Though perhaps they should be renamed "Survive" or "Hang in there."

Snacks: Almonds. Cashews. Popcorn. Cheese. Baby carrots.

Restaurant food: "I ate out to treat myself," one BWC member recalls. "I figured, this man is treating me badly, so I will treat myself well to try and even up the balance."

EMDR

EMDR, which stands for Eye Movement Desensitization and Reprocessing, seems a bit like hocus-pocus. A trained therapist talks you through traumatic experiences while either guiding your eyes in a repetitive back-and-forth or rhythmically tapping on your hands or legs. Some use a buzzer.

It's a relatively new therapy developed by an American psychotherapist named Francine Shapiro, who noticed that when walking, her own distressing memories became less so. She assumed it was the eye movements one makes when walking, a sort of scanning, that were desensitizing. She dug into her observation and discovered that others with post-trauma symptoms were similarly helped.

The idea, my therapist explained, is to access memory stored as trauma and, essentially, refile it in a part of the brain that feels a greater control over the experience. The website of the EMDR Institute describes it as removing a block that's in the way of emotional healing.

However it's described, I couldn't quite believe it worked. I felt lighter than I'd felt in years. Free of so much sadness. Liberated from so much self-blame.

Better than that, I could also re-access positive emotions. As my therapist explained, when we put the lid on pain in order to avoid feeling it, we also bottle up everything else, like joy and contentment. We don't get to be selective in what we bury and what we don't. By going back in and wrestling with the pain, I created an opening for all that good stuff too.

EMDR has its detractors. There are those who call it pseudoscience. But count me among the converts. If you can't afford it (and it can be expensive), get out and walk every day. There's evidence that the bilateral stimulation of walking can also excavate those buried feelings, letting them bubble to the surface where you can process them, reminding yourself that you're safe now, that you are strong enough to handle pain. And knowing that behind that pain lies a world of rich color and emotion that's worth fighting for.

Emotional Affairs

There are women who often apologize for coming to the Betrayed Wives Club site because their husbands "only" had an emotional affair.

Only?

My father "only" had an emotional affair, but it unmoored my formerly invincible mother enough to launch her into a decade-long alcoholic-and-prescription-drug stupor. He never could quite get why she was so affected by it. My mom and I talked a lot about it as adults because that one event, quite literally, altered the trajectory of our lives.

And that, my friends, is what affairs do – whether they involve torrid sex, tepid sex or no sex at all. They are a trust violation, which is the worst form of betrayal.

So to all those of you who are beating yourselves up for being completely unhinged by "only" an emotional affair, I say you need to look at the situation as a trust violation and recognize that such a betrayal is devastating, no matter the details.

And don't apologize for your pain. Anyone with blood coursing in their veins is going to feel like hell when they discover an affair. Even if it's "only" an emotional affair.

Escape Plan, Why You Need An

An Escape Plan is a step-by-step plan of what you'll do if...

A) Your husband won't end his affair or is lying about ending the affair.

B) He engages in the crazy-making behaviour common to cheating husbands, including but not limited to calling you hysterical, out-of-control, jealous, manipulative, or he otherwise makes YOU the problem.

C) He uses divorce as his trump card, as in, "If you can't just leave the past in the past then we should just divorce."

An Escape Plan is about taking back your life and controlling your future. You may never act on your Escape Plan but it's paramount to your healing to have a plan that focuses on your well-being.

How do you create an Escape Plan?

•Start by figuring out where you would go if you needed short-term accommodation. It might be your parents' house, a best friend's, a neighbor's. We're simply thinking short-term here, somewhere you could go to escape for a few days or a week, taking kids if necessary, in order to get your head straight and/or allow your spouse to get his head straight and, perhaps, recognize that the New You isn't going to tolerate his bullshit.

•Work out what logistics need to be in place: For example, if your short-term accommodation involves leaving town, how will this affect getting to your job or getting kids to school? Can you commute for a few days or weeks? Is there somewhere else the kids would need to stay during the week? Would a nearby hotel be a better option?

•Ensure access to cash: Do you have a bank account? A credit card that he can't cancel? What if your short-term turns into a month or longer?

•Meet with a lawyer to determine what your life would look like if you left the marriage. This is just a dress rehearsal. It's a chance for you to assume more power in your life and be clear on what you're entitled to financially, how property would be divided up and what custody might look like for your children.

Your Escape Plan is as much an insurance policy as an actual plan. It's something to have considered in case things get more hellish. In case he cheats again. In case his affair never ended. In case the Other Woman announces she's pregnant. It's to ensure you can respond even if you're reeling. And it's to offer you some security that even if you don't get blindsided again...you'd be prepared if you were.

Exercise

Along with "wait," among the most common advice from the Betrayed Wives of BWC is "exercise." We know, of course, that exercise does all sorts of good stuff for our brains – greasing the wheels of the feel-good hormones while slowing down the "I hate life" hormones. But exercise will also remind you of something important: You are strong. And you will get stronger.

Whether or not exercise means walking your dog to the end of the street or whether it means signing up for a kick-boxing class where you pretend that your sparring partner is the Other Woman and unleash your inner Ronda Rousey, exercise is key to moving through the pain of betrayal.

I ran. I would hit the streets after dark when nobody could see the tears streaming down my cheeks, and I would run through the rage and the sadness and the revenge fantasies. Not only did it help me process a whole lot of emotion but it reminded me that I needed to take care of myself. And exercise is a big part of that.

Expectations, How to Manage Your

The day I turned nine was perfect. I awoke the morning after, went downstairs before anyone else was awake, and recreated the entire birthday. I rewrapped my presents. I gathered up the kitten I'd been given the day before (a kitten!). And I felt that same sense of excitement and anticipation and delight that I'd felt the day before.

By my 12th birthday, my mother had abandoned any party planning. I invited a few friends over, cooked hot dogs, bought myself a cake in the frozen section of the grocery store. My mother, drunk but also sick with laryngitis, spent the entire party ringing a dinner bell to summon me to her bed to get her a drink of water or to fluff her pillows. My friends exchanged looks. My helpless fury mounted. I begged her to stop and let me just be with my friends. They left shortly after and I stewed in my humiliation.

I've had a lot of birthdays since then. And for way too many years, I've been disappointed. However, as my old therapist would remind me, if your feelings are bigger than the situation calls for, it's always about old stuff.

My birthday is old stuff.

And yet...I can't seem to let go of those expectations.

For one day, I want it to be about me. For one day, I want people to spoil me. Just one day.

And though my family knows that this occasion takes place Every. Single. Year. On. The. Same. Day. They can't seem to get their acts together to buy a card, bake a cake, choose a gift (or make one! I'm not picky! It mustn't always be a kitten!).

Over the years, I've worked to accept reality. And I know my expectations are about old stuff.

And so I organize something annually to mark my birthday. I sometimes make our dinner reservations. I often buy all the ingredients for a cake and simply announce that "at some point, I would like a cake."

I've come a long way.

I've learned that, rather than nurse those resentments, to give myself what I need. What I need is to feel valued. And so I value myself.

It can look different depending on the year. I might buy myself an outfit that I'd otherwise tell myself I didn't need. I might take the day away from my computer. I might sit outside in the gorgeous sunshine and read a few chapters of a book. I ignore that little voice that says I should be doing something productive, like making money or taking care of someone.

I am taking care of someone. Myself.

It has taken me more than five decades to see the value in the simple act of taking care of myself. The value in not letting resentments gain a foothold.

My family loves me. I know this. They show me in many ways, none of which involve having a cake made on time, or carefully chosen gifts.

Instead they show me with last-minute promises, like my son's card that told me I'm the best mom "ever" and that he'll take me to lunch and then to the store that sells my favorite yoga pants and will buy me "anything." With homemade cards that, though created out of necessity more than desire, nonetheless are more beautiful than anything off the card rack.

Managing my expectations continues to be a challenge for me. People disappoint me all the time. But as I learn to go easier on myself, I'm able to go easier on others. It's not the same as letting people off the hook for bad behaviour. Rather it's about not expecting everyone to think and act like me. It's about letting them be who they are and to love me in their own way.

But mostly it's about getting clear about what I need and then finding a way to deliver it to myself. That's what being a grown up is about.

It's something I seemed to understand on that ninth birthday. That, even the day after, I was able to give myself what I needed, to remind myself that I matter. And, for the record, what I almost always need involves a cat.

F

❧

Forgiveness

Brené Brown tells us that embedded deeply in forgiveness is grief.

Think about that.

I always thought of forgiveness as something that people who weren't burdened with resentment and anger offered freely, then moved blithely into the rest of their lives. It took me years to realize that forgiveness doesn't work like that, especially when the transgression is deep and painful.

I wondered what was wrong with me that, even with my husband apologizing around the clock for his betrayal of me, I refused to grant forgiveness. Those people who had forgiven their spouse must be more spiritually evolved than I, I figured. They must simply be better people. Or maybe they were idiots.

There were times in those early days that I didn't hate my husband, which felt a teensy bit like forgiveness. But mostly, I cried and simmered in resentment. I wasn't ready to leave but I hated staying. Forgiveness? Didn't that mean I was putting all this behind us? Didn't that mean I was okay with what he did? Didn't that mean I could never bring it up again?

Forget that.

So many years later, have I now forgiven my husband? I confess I'm not sure what that means. I'm with him and happy to be. I trust him as much as I trust anyone who has revealed themselves capable of deception, which is the same as saying, I trust him as much as I trust anyone. His cheating is part of our story but only part. We rarely speak about it. I no longer use it like a sword, a way to cut him when I'm hurting.

Forgiveness though?

Maybe.

I've grieved, which is a key part of forgiveness. Something definitely died when I was betrayed. A lot of somethings. My sense of safety. My idea of who he was. My idea of what my marriage was. My dream of doing marriage "right" (which says a whole lot about me, which I've had to wrestle with). My "perfect" family. A veritable graveyard of dreams.

And I had to grieve it all. Year by year. Tear by tear.

So maybe I have landed in this place of forgiveness. I've accepted that my husband is more than the worst thing he ever did. I admire and respect how hard he's worked to become a better person, how painful it was for him to face down his own demons. Plenty died for him too. His fantasy of his perfect childhood. The myth he'd constructed of his father. He had his own grieving to do.

We've both come to understand that forgiveness comes *only* after grieving. We are cheating ourselves when we use forgiveness as a balm for our pain, as an attempt to erase what's happened to us.

Forgiveness trips up a lot of us who cannot imagine extending it and yet feel as though it's required in order to heal. But maybe we're looking at it wrong. Maybe forgiveness isn't something we bestow but rather something that is bestowed on us when we've worked through our grief. Maybe it's not something we feel but rather a place we arrive.

I had always thought forgiveness came easily to those more emotionally generous and loving than I. Now I know it's the product of blood, sweat, tears and time. It comes when we validate our own pain and grieve the loss of the life we thought we had, the man we thought he was.

If you aren't sure whether you can forgive, then put it aside. You needn't submit a forgiveness card before you can pass through the mythological gates to healing.

But one day, you might discover that the past no longer casts its shadow and that, you might say, is forgiveness.

FRIEND, WHEN HE CHEATS WITH A

By Iris, member of the Betrayed Wives Club:

Dear Doubly Betrayed Wife,

When this happened to a friend of mine involving a close family friend of long-standing, my friend told mutual acquaintances why the two couples would no longer be socialising. She wondered what reasons they'd think up for a sudden split and she preferred to be honest. It did mean that she had a lot of support from those around her, rather as if there had been a bereavement. And many of us were able to support her and her husband when we saw how remorseful he was and how hard he worked to understand his behaviour and make amends. There will always be casualties as far as friendships go when betrayals like this happen, but asking for help is one way of finding out who your real friends are.

Make sure you're not isolated. Remember these were your husband's choices – they don't reflect poorly on you. I know it can feel as if they do.

As for the best friend – there can hardly be a worse betrayal of trust. We expect so much more. I would hate her too. But hate is such a heavy burden for you to carry. It doesn't help that there's a commonly held idea that somehow only the cheating spouse is to blame, as if we shouldn't have anger toward someone who has violated our boundaries in the worst possible way. In your case she knows intimately the people who will suffer through her behaviour. We're supposed to be somehow 'dignified' about this.

One of the five precepts of mindfulness is helpful here (and mindfulness generally can be very helpful – as someone who breaks the other precepts by drinking alcohol, eating meat and killing clothes moths, so don't worry about MY spiritual superiority). This is by a lovely man, a Buddhist monk called Thich Nhat Hanh:

'Sexual expression should not take place without love and commitment. Be fully aware of the sufferings you may cause others as a result of your misconduct. To preserve the happiness of yourself and others, respect the rights and commitments of others."

This is not just Buddhist; it is universal. It is the right medicine for our illness. 'I will do everything in my power to prevent couples and families being broken by sexual misconduct.'

We should all 'respect the rights and commitments of others' out of basic decency, and we should ask that others do so too. It needn't be a question of outdated morality suggesting property rights, but an understanding that we're all responsible for each other and especially for the well-being of children. I see it as a humanist stance. Be confident that there's nothing wrong with your continued suffering, it's understandable, and extend compassion to yourself for being placed in a position (like so many others) of feeling anger toward someone you trusted and liked. You didn't seek out this hatred.

She has caused you a great deal of pain but much more damage to herself. Even if no one points out to her how badly she's behaved (and personally I don't think that would be a bad thing) she will have to carry the consequences of her actions for the rest of her life. No karma required. You can let your anger wear itself out with time and you can be stronger trusting that for all the faults you do have, as we all do, you haven't abandoned integrity and kindness. She will have to work very hard to recover the integrity she's lost, whether she understands this now or has yet to realize. I wouldn't want to experience such remorse.

I suppose the bottom line is that you can't make yourself forget (I think I would move to a different house, but that's another issue). You have to learn to hold yourself through this ordeal, to breathe through it, to not lose yourself. It could be the making of you.

Friends, Should You Tell Your (See also Circle of Trust)

By Laura S., member of Betrayed Wives Club and founder of Infidelity Counseling Network:

The week after my husband told me he thought he was in love with someone else, I e-mailed some close girlfriends with the news. The next evening they stopped their busy-kids-husbands-making-dinner-supervising-homework lives and met me at a local café where we drank tea and I wept. They listened.

After that night, I decided to tell others. Everyone. Anyone. Friends, my family, his family, co-workers, the woman in front of me at the supermarket, the moms of my daughter's friends. I thought that if I told enough people, it wouldn't hurt so much. No one would blame me. They would nod knowingly when we got divorced (or when I kicked him out, which I inevitably did, in my rage. He came back).

Soon after hearing the news, friends and family reacted in ways that told me more about them and infidelity than about me. My closest girlfriends (all married) phoned to tell me they loved me and were here for me. An invisible army out beyond my house where I couldn't see them. Rows and rows of people who supported me, waiting there to hold me in their arms if I needed holding or walk with me to happiness when I was ready to walk.

My mom, in an atypical expression of outward emotion, told me she would be there for whether we got divorced or stayed married. A few friends, male and female, told me they'd happily kill, maim or strangle my husband (one sounded uncomfortably serious). A couple of friends admitted they were so angry with him that they didn't know how they were going to work through that (they are still struggling, I think, because their manner is different around him now). One friend never mentioned it, not for the entire five months of the affair nor the following two years of recovery; to this date she does not bring it up or ask me how I am.

I know that my story – and telling everyone so openly and forcefully – was terrifying to many of our friends. 'If this could happen to her, could it happen to me?' went the unstated refrain. 'Would my husband do this? Is he capable of such a choice?' No one ever spoke those words but they were there. My experience was a threat, something "other" that loomed on the edge of our nice middle-class world.

There was more. While this support was so key to my survival, there was something missing. No one said, 'Hey, I've been there.' No one ventured, 'My sister has been through this.' I felt as if I was the only human on earth whose husband had betrayed her. Of course I'd heard about infidelity – in movies and books, with celebrities and politicians – but I did not know anyone else like me who had been through it. Feeling so uniquely marked in this way was like a scarlet 'I' (for infidelity) worn on my forehead for an entire year. It was only later, once we began to rebuild our relationship and I started sharing with people too about that effort, that three girlfriends came to me with their own infidelity stories. Finally, I was not alone.

Friends To Avoid After His Affair

I told very few friends about my husband's affair because I could barely process it. One friend I did confide in, largely because her own marriage had been marked by infidelity and I thought she'd understand, was dismissive, which only compounded my sense of isolation and pain.

It can add to our pain, to learn that someone we counted on simply can't or won't be there for us. The friend who dismissed my pain was eventually – years later – able to acknowledge that she had let me down. She admitted that she was so blinded by her own pain and her choice to leave her marriage that she wasn't able to accept my choice to not leave.

Another friend, not then a close one but someone who worked with my husband and his assistant (with whom my husband was having an affair), became a pillar of support for me. (She discovered for herself two years later just how devastating betrayal is.)

It's when we're on our knees that we discover just who in our lives will kneel alongside us.

Not all friends will get to that point. Not all friends are, well, friends.

For instance...

•There's the "friend" who uses your husband's behaviour as an excuse to cut you off. "I just can't be around you right now. I can't even look at your husband." Suddenly your pain is about her discomfort.

•There's the "friend" who compounds your loneliness because infidelity terrifies her. "I just can't imagine my husband doing such a thing." She's right. She can't imagine. And won't let herself because it might mean facing some uncomfortable truths, such as, even good marriages can be affected by infidelity.

•There's the "friend" who knows better than you do what your right path is. "Once a cheater, always a cheater. You need to kick him out." Her cynicism and bitterness and, perhaps, her fear that you'll get hurt again and she can't protect you, leads her to encourage you to do what she wants you to do, instead of allowing you to find your own path.

•There's the "friend" who minimizes what your husband has done because she's cheated on her spouse. "All marriages come up against this. You need to let it go. He picked you, didn't he?" Seeing the devastation of infidelity up close brings up a lot of guilt.

•And there's the "friend," like mine, who encourages you to leave your husband because that's what she did. "I don't know why anyone would stay. I certainly couldn't." Accepting that it's possible for a marriage to heal from betrayal can make those who chose to leave – and aren't 100% sure of their choice – wonder if they made the wrong choice. My friend ultimately copped to this, admitting that she left her ex because she thought that was her only choice. She saw no models of anyone who'd stayed and made it work because nobody ever talked about that choice. Our cultural narrative rarely supports the healing/rebuilding option. And admittedly, it's tough. Really tough.

It can help to have a true friend who's willing to hold you up while you figure out which way to go. Someone who's there to hold your hand through the bad days and celebrate the good ones. Someone who is in your life because he or she deserves to be there. Even friends who don't know what you're going through can offer much support in the form of distraction or small kindnesses. Their presence is enough.

I often think of my post-betrayal life as one that has been curated by me. I'm more discerning about how I spend my time (I've added the word "no" to my vocabulary as in, "thanks so much for asking but 'no,' I won't be available to bake 350 cookies for your bake sale on Thursday." Or simply 'no.' (See **No**). I'm more careful about those who are in my life. Gone are the "friends" who made passive-aggressive comments. Gone are those who were suddenly absent when my life fell apart. Gone are the gossips. Gone are the fair-weather friends. And you know what? I don't miss them.

Not in the least.

G

Gaslighting, What is

In 1938, a play debuted in London's West End, in which a character named Bella Manningham is terrorized by her husband Jack. Jack hides household items while blaming Bella for misplacing them. He tells her she's imagining the footsteps in the supposedly empty upstairs apartment, even though the footsteps are his as he searches for the missing jewels of the former murdered tenant. The lights Jack turns on in the upstairs apartment to help him search cause the lights in his apartment with Bella to dim and it is this that Bella clings to as proof that she's not going insane.

Gaslighting entered pop culture lexicon as a buzzy word for what is manipulation and emotional abuse. It refers colloquially to an alternate reality in which one person is told that she can't trust her eyes, her ears or, especially, her intuition. It is one partner manipulating another into believing she's going crazy.

There are times, of course, when we're not actually victims of gaslighting. When the lunch with a co-worker really is innocent. When coming home late really is because of an accident that tied up traffic.

But there are times, oh don't we all know it too well, when we're right but being told we're wrong. When we're told that those texts don't mean anything when they definitely do. When we're chastised for being nosy even as we're turning up proof that he's lying. When we're told we're the crazy ones.

Challenge that with every ounce of strength you have. Challenge anyone who responds to your suspicion with empty platitudes or who turns it against you. Challenge anyone whose response to your genuine fear of betrayal is anything other than, *what do you need from me to trust me? Let's work together to build trust in each other.*

Glass, Shirley

Shirley Glass is something of an icon in the world of infidelity, hailed by *The New York Times* as "the godmother of infidelity research." She brought her background as a clinical psychologist to her subject matter and was one of the first to notice that, as more women entered the workforce, friendships among men and women shifted, leading to an increase in the number of women cheating and to more workplace affairs. It's a trend we've seen shift further still with the advent of social media, which, of course, makes cheating (including online affairs/sexting) as common as dirt. Dr. Glass's research, along with two decades of working with couples dealing with infidelity, led to the release of her seminal book "Not Just Friends." Fifteen years later, it remains relevant and is often cited as one of the first books women read when they learn of a partner's affair.

H

❦

Hook, Am I Letting Him Off the

It feels like something of a miracle following D-Day. Something makes us laugh and, for a moment, we forget that our life is a wreck. Or maybe we wake up one morning and the boulder on our chest feels a little less heavy.

Or perhaps our husband comes home to find us colouring with our preschooler and soaking up her innocence.

We almost smile at him. Then we remember: He's the enemy.

Navigating those first few months is hell. Even if we've decided to stay in the marriage (for the time being, anyway), even if we're engaged in hysterical bonding (see also **Hysterical Bonding**), even if we can't imagine life without him, we can feel as though we're on opposing sides. We are loathe to, as we think of it, let him off the hook.

And what is the hook?

The hook is this misery he has cast us into. The hook is this heart of ours he has shattered. This life he took a wrecking ball to.

The hook is our fear that, if we even for a minute behave as if we're not utterly ruined, he might just think that what he did was okay.

And it was decidedly NOT okay.

It will never be okay.

But let's stop for a second and consider this mindset.

Do we really think that, without a constant reminder of the destruction he has wrought, our husband might think that he's off the hook?

Because, frankly, maintaining a look of agony, day-in and day-out for the rest of our lives in order to ensure that our husband knows he is not off the hook sounds exhausting. It sounds like manipulation. Not in the short term, of course, when we really do feel shattered. But eventually.

I remember the feeling well. I remember worrying that if I actually started feeling better and, more to the point, acting as if I was feeling better, that my husband might mop his sweaty brow, breathe a sigh of relief and think to himself, "Whew. Glad that's over and I can get back to my job of ignoring her pain and doing whatever I want regardless of the impact to my marriage or her."

I might not have put it in exactly those terms. More likely, I thought of it as, if I reveal that I'm healing then he will think he's off the hook. And he is not. He will never be.

And that has remained true.

Though it has been many years since D-Day, my husband is not off the hook. No matter that I now laugh, that I go days or weeks without thinking about his former infidelity at all, that I feel grateful to have him in my life, he is still not and never will be off the hook.

He knows that.

He knows that I can love my life and still never be okay with his cheating. He knows that healing from his betrayal will never make his betrayal okay. And he knows that, having been given the gift of a second chance by me, he would be a fool to ask for a third chance.

And so...I was free to heal. You are too.

You are free to laugh when something is funny. You are free to smile when you feel happy. You are free to feel whatever you might feel in the moment without forfeiting your right to NOT be okay with his betrayal of you. To never be okay about it.

You don't need to remain miserable in order to ensure his fidelity.

You can speak to him about it. Like an adult.

You can share your feelings with him. You can share just how difficult it is to heal from this and what a miracle it feels to be able to laugh again, to have a glimpse of a life that isn't utterly darkened by betrayal.

And, if he is a good, decent man doing the hard work of understanding why he made the indecent choice he did, he will listen to you. He will do his best to understand. He won't ever be okay with what he did either. He will always know that pain he caused. As my husband once said, the worst feeling in his life was seeing the pain in my eyes and knowing he had caused it.

If your husband has really acknowledged what he did and taken responsibility then he will think your laughter is the most beautiful sound in the world, not because it lets him off the hook but because it sounds like hope.

Hope doesn't erase the past. It opens the heart to the future.

Hysterical Bonding

Otherwise known as "why the hell do I want sex with my unfaithful husband?", hysterical bonding refers to the surprisingly common phenomenon following discovery of a spouse's adultery to suddenly crave sex with that person morning, noon and night. And though it's called "hysterical bonding," there's nothing funny about it. I confess (TMI coming...this is your warning), I gave my husband a blow-job within a half-hour of learning he'd cheated on me.

WTF? At the time, it seemed I was like a dog staking out my territory. We then proceeded to indulge in weeks of wild and incredible sexual escapades.

Then, as quickly as it appeared, it vanished, leaving a shaking, incoherent, grief-stricken me wondering what the hell that was all about. And, by the way, *ewwwww...*

According to the experts, many couples dealing with infidelity engage in hysterical bonding, in part as a path toward intimacy and reconciliation. While there's still a LOT of work to be done, it does get the ball rolling – so to speak.

It can, however, leave the betrayed spouse feeling bewildered and perhaps betrayed by her own body. *How can I want him?* we wonder.

Part of it can be a desperate attempt to lure him back to us, a sort of siren call, which, because it won't work with someone deep in the fog of his affair, leaves us feeling pathetic and rejected further.

It might also be about reclaiming what we feel is ours, kinda like clubbing him on the head and dragging him back to our cave (the clubbing on the head part is very tempting. Refrain.). Or it can also be our way of soothing ourselves. Betrayal is traumatizing by anyone's estimation. And with trauma comes a primal way of seeking comfort. It can seem very disconcerting to be seeking comfort in the arms of the very person who betrayed us. But, if reconciliation is even on your radar, it makes sense to turn to that person.

Whatever the reason, it's a reality for many couples. Just

one caveat: Use protection, i.e. a condom. This guy might swear he always used them during his affair(s). Or that they only kissed. Your husband isn't exactly the Dalai Lama at this point in time so I wouldn't trust a whole lot of what he says. The only way to be sure he's clean is testing. In the meantime, protect yourself.

I

Individual Counselling

I don't know anyone who has survived betrayal without finding a therapist or some support (pastor, support group, social worker) though I know plenty who've tried. And though marriage counselling has its place, I think you also need your own therapist to support you through this. You need an objective listener whose sole goal is to help you navigate the worst pain of your life, someone whose goal isn't to keep you married but keep you sane.

Not all therapists are created alike, unfortunately. While I was lucky to find a compassionate female therapist who walked the perfect line between totally accepting me and challenging my sometimes wacky thinking (and who also was covered 100% by insurance), I've heard far too many stories of therapists who wonder aloud why you're not "over it" in three months, or who encourage you to "let it go" or "try to understand his point of view." There's a time and place for letting go, getting over it and trying to see his point of view, of course. But it's not until you've firmly established a relationship with this therapist and are convinced that he/she has your best interests at heart.

Seek the person who can support you as you work through the pain of betrayal. A safe place where you can rant and rage but where you will also heal, not forever cast as a victim. It's kinda like dating. If the first one doesn't work out, try another. And another. If, after three, you still don't think you've found "the one," it might be you, not her/him.

Therapists are, of course, not cheap. Churches can sometimes step in if they have the benefit of a particularly wise pastor but, just as often I fear, they subscribe to a "stay married at all costs" that minimizes your pain and makes the marriage more important than the sin. There are support groups out there, so Google your heart out to see if there's anything in your area. If you have the energy, create your own.

Infidelity Diet (see also Eat, What to)

Sometimes also called The Divorce Diet, this is a weight-loss plan that isn't really planned. Instead, it's the consequence of being too heartbroken, too distraught, too emotionally wrung out to eat. And though it's effective, it's not very healthy. Fortunately (or unfortunately, depending on your point of view), within a few months or so, your appetite will return, along with your curves.

Inside an Affair

A few years ago, a betrayed wife posted this on the Betrayed Wives Club:

A little insight into how the other woman feels. This was from a friend who doesn't know that I've been betrayed. I knew about her affair partner but I'm ashamed to say I only took an interest once it had happened to me and the fact that we didn't catch up much as we were thousands of miles away.

Week one of her affair: They met at a convention. Drinks after the meeting, mutual attraction. She was single, he was married, which she knew. Ended up in bed by the end of the week. She told me of the flattery: He'd 'never had sex like it,' she was 'the most beautiful woman' he had ever seen, she 'got him.'

Weeks 2 and 3. He went to her apartment for dinner and more sex. Took her some flowers and champagne. He opened up more about his wife, how the marriage was dead, and he was only staying for the kids.

Months 2 and 3. They meet at least three or four times a week. He has now told her he loves her. He can't stand being without her. She is having the time of her life. Dressing up, being admired, little gifts. I tell her to watch out. Her heart will be broken. And doesn't she think of his wife and kids? Yes, she did, says she felt terrible at first but now she realises they 'were meant to be' and besides, the wife is a real ogre, moans all the time, they sleep in separate rooms.

Months 4 and 5. Still going well and she still adores him. Bit upset he couldn't spend her birthday with her, and she was hoping to take a little holiday with him. She gives him the key in case he can turn up or if the old bag of a wife gives him too much grief he can spend some time at her apartment. After all, he will probably be moving in one day.

Months 6 and 7. She tells me she's getting a bit pissed about the situation. She really thought by now he would be putting some plans into place about leaving, you know, stashing some money in a different account for when he moves. She finds out the family are going on holiday together. Why would he do that when he can't stand her? Well, you know, united front for the kids and all that.

Months 8 and 9. He has started cancelling a few times. Still says he loves her and they will be together one day. She's had to keep him secret from her friends, so she's missing out on her social life.

Months 9 and 10. She decides to do a drive-by past his house.

WTF, there he is in the front garden with the ogre of a wife, who quite frankly would give Julia Roberts a run for her money. How can he be laughing with her? She doesn't tell him she went by the house. Actually, he never told her exactly where he lived but she found out one day from his wallet. He always told her his wife never had Facebook. Oh dear, big mistake, especially when the photos are public. That holiday that was only for the kids, well, there was an awful lot of affection going on, and what was that picture taken at Christmas of the whole family on the bed opening presents? Then a close-up picture of the gorgeous eternity ring he bought her. She had never seen him look so happy.

Cut to the present day. She confronted him. Told him he had to make his mind up. That she wasn't going to wait. He apologized and said sorry, she was lovely but he did love his wife and his head was turned. Begged her not to tell his wife.

It cut like a knife hearing her story, I wanted to shout 'You bitch, how could you?' But when she cried on my shoulder and said she felt such a fool, used and abused, he was stringing me along all the time. She said that she felt inferior to the wife and the compliments meant nothing as she knew they were just words to get her into bed.

The final piece of her humiliation: My friend, the OW, went to a book club organized by a friend of a friend. And yes, his wife was one of the members. After a few weeks of being in the same room, she hears one evening after a few glasses of wine what a great sex life this woman has with her husband. She seems happy. My friend said she wanted to destroy her happiness that evening by blurting out the truth. She hasn't so far.

J

Journaling

I was nine when I first began a diary. Writing quickly became the way I made sense of the world, from the mundane to the devastating. I wrote about too much homework, a fight with my brother, I crappy friends and crappier boyfriends. Year after year, notebook after notebook, I wrote.

Marriage and kids and life got busy. Daily entries gave way to weekly or monthly. Or bi-annually. Writing was my career so I didn't feel the same pull to write as a hobby. Or as therapy.

Then came betrayal. And with it, anger and shame and humiliation and a seemingly bottomless sorrow.

I picked up a notebook and started writing.

I wrote about my anger and shame and humiliation and profound sadness.

I said all the things I couldn't quite bring myself to say to real flesh-and-blood people.

I spewed hatred and fury and thoughts of revenge. I

spilled my agony onto those pages, which somehow shored me up enough to contain it the rest of the time. Mostly.

Writing through the pain saved me. It allowed me an outlet for the hugeness of the feelings that I thought would swallow me.

It allowed me to see, when I read earlier pages, that I was actually moving forward. That, though I felt raw and ragged, I wasn't as raw and ragged as a few days or weeks ago.

"If I don't write to empty my mind," said Lord Byron, "I would go mad."

Dean Koontz acknowledged that "Writing is a form of therapy; sometimes I wonder how all those, who do not write...can manage to escape the madness, the melancholia, the panic fear, which is inherent in a human condition."

I believe I would have gone mad, but for the ability to put my madness on the page.

Those diaries exist in a Rubbermaid container in a dark corner of my basement. I sometimes worry that I will get hit by a bus and my children will stumble on them at some point in the future, open the cover and discover that their mother had many secrets.

Perhaps sometime soon I will host a bonfire of my insanities, warming my hands over the flames as my words become ash.

For now, I write.

"Just show up"

I was a worrier. I worried that I wouldn't get invited to the party. That I wouldn't get the job. Or I *would* get the job but I wouldn't know where the bathroom was and I might get lost and then everybody at my new job would hate me. I worried that they had given me the job because they mistakenly thought me more capable than I was. I worried that I was a bad mother because my first child cried incessantly. I worried that I was a bad mother because my third child never bothered crying at all. I worried at author readings that nobody would show up. I worried that they would show up and would leave disappointed.

Over decades, I communicated all this worry to my mother, who would listen patiently before, inevitably, giving me her advice. "Just show up, sweetie," she would say. "That's all you can do."

It was stupid advice, I thought. What the hell did "just show up" mean? I was showing up. All I ever did was show up, albeit after agonizing over whether I was wearing the right shoes or the right lipstick or had prepared the right work.

And then D-Day hit me a week before the final chapter was due on a book and it was all I could do to drag myself to a computer to finish the final few pages. And then, six months later, my mother passed away suddenly the night before my book was released to the world.

The morning after my mother passed away, I was scheduled to do an hour-long phone interview with a radio station. It didn't feel right to cancel on such short notice so, with four hours of sleep behind me and a huge cup of tea in front of me, I dialled in. I talked about my book and why I wrote it and what I hoped it meant to readers. And when I hung up the phone an hour later, I realized that I hadn't worried about what I was saying or whether they liked me or if I measured up. I had shown up, which was all I was capable of at that moment. And I got it. It was like my mother, whose eyes had closed for the final time just hours earlier, was whispering in my ear. "Just show up, sweetie."

Over the next weeks and months and years, I was called way out of my comfort zone to do radio programs, television interviews, speaking engagements, all while reeling from betrayal and my mom's death. And I would hear my mom's voice before I exhaled and just showed up.

I continue to just show up in so many ways. It feels like carrying my mom in my heart, of moving through the world the way she'd always wanted for me. And I tell my own children to just show up. I don't think they yet know exactly what it means. But the world will test them. I hope they remember the answer.

Juicy

A friend recently referred to a 40-plus year old woman, who would NOT be confused with a supermodel, as "juicy." And I loved it. She was juicy. She exuded a confidence and a sexuality that had nothing to do with size 0 jeans and perky breasts.

So I'm telling myself lately that I'm "juicy." That my husband didn't cheat because I wear cotton briefs or have stretch marks or back fat. I'm remembering that sex isn't about gymnastics but pleasure. It's about feeling juicy.

K

Kindness, Random Acts of

I was moved by a story that one of our secret sisters at Betrayed Wives Club shared, hoping to encourage other random acts of kindness. This betrayed wife had rediscovered running in the wake of her husband's infidelity, a pastime that she found enormously healing. She wanted another betrayed wife to have the chance to experience the power of pounding the pavement, so she purchased a gift card for a local sports store, that she asked her therapist to give to another betrayed wife who might benefit from taking up running.

I love that this woman, even in the midst of her own heartbreak, created a way to bridge the space to another's heartbreak.

Extending kindness to others, especially when we know their pain, can help us heal our own. It can remind us of the goodness in the world and that we can tap into it too.

L

❧

Letter to a Husband Who Cheated

Dear He-Who-Cheated,

I get letter upon letter from women who are desperate to be heard in the wake of your betrayal. And over and over again they tell me that you won't talk to them about it, won't go to therapy with them, don't understand why they're not "over it."

You want to know why we want – why we *need* – to talk about it? Because you shattered our faith in you as a decent, honest man, and the only way we can reconcile our desire to stay with you with our knowledge that you lied and cheated and violated your vows is to try, as best we can, to understand just how you could do that and still be someone worthy of our love. We're begging you to help us love you again. And the best most of you can do is ask, aloud, why we aren't over it.

There isn't a betrayed wife who doesn't desperately wish she could be over it. We're not a bunch of masochists, revelling in our pain, compulsively picking away at the wound. We are women who are experiencing more pain than we ever imagined.

A lot of us had, perhaps, wondered abstractedly what we might do if our husbands cheated. I always thought I'd just be pissed off. I figured I'd get angry, show him the door and that would be the end of it.

I never *ever* imagined how emotionally crippled I would be by the realization that my husband had cheated on me. I just never imagined it. Anger? Hell yeah. But a pain so deep I could hardly breathe? Wasn't expecting that.

Psychologists and marriage therapists aren't surprised. They've seen how damaging what they term "trust violations" are. They've seen what a deep primal wound it causes. It's no coincidence that children who experience trust violations, if they aren't given help to heal, go on to experience the world as a terrifying place. In fact, many therapists insist that often what they see in partners who've been betrayed are symptoms of post-traumatic stress. Free-floating anxiety. Fear of what could happen. A lack of trust in our ability to handle things. A feeling of numbness. Sudden rage or terror. Sounds an awful lot like your wife after learning of your affair, doesn't it? And though many of us get better at managing those emotions, the best way to eliminate them is to process them.

And we do that by telling our story. Sometimes over and over again. And we need you to listen. To answer our questions, even if you've already told us (it's amazing how foggy our brains are post-betrayal).

I know it's hard. I know it requires you repeatedly owning up to just how shitty you feel. We know you feel shitty. But that doesn't change how *we* feel. It just makes this about you and your feelings instead of about us and our feelings. It requires a really brave man who can admit his shortcomings. Who can face that he made a choice that devastated the one person he promised never to devastate. It means doing the hard work of figuring out just what story you were telling yourself that made cheating okay. And figuring just what part of that story still needs addressing. You don't feel heard in your marriage? That's legitimate. Talk to her about it. You feel like little more than an ATM for your family? Not uncommon. Talk to them about it. But talk about it *after* you've dressed her wound, so to speak. She can't hear you and your pain when she's metaphorically bleeding all over the floor.

Tell her that nothing she did made what *you* did okay. That you hate that you were that guy. That you are doing everything you can to never be that guy again. That you know how hard it is for her to give you a second chance but that you are going to spend every day of your life deserving it.

Hold her, if that's what she needs. Listen to her, if that's what she needs. Pour her a bath, if that's what she needs.

And know that you may need to do that again tomorrow night. And the night after that.

But please also know that, the more you do this now, the stronger she'll become. It's like depositing into a bank account now and letting the interest accrue to enjoy it later.

Now will be hell. I get that. Just when you want to forget about this, she wants to go over it. Again.

She's not doing it to punish you. She's not doing it to hurt you. She's doing it because her brain is trying to process something confusing and excruciating. She's doing it to figure out what little clue she missed so that she can be sure she never misses it again. Sometimes she's doing it because she saw something that day that triggered her pain in that deep, dark place. And she felt vulnerable and scared, which often gets masked by anger.

She's doing it to heal.

So please, don't dismiss her pain. Don't insist that she should be "over this by now."

The good news? It seems counter-intuitive but the more you talk about it and validate her pain, the more quickly she'll move through it. She'll be better able to replace those fears with the assurance that you're there for her. Maybe not then...but now. Now you are.

Betrayal changes everything. And while you can't undo what you did, you can take steps to show that you've learned from it. That you're a better man than that. That she's worth going through hell for. And, now, so are you.

Signed,
A Betrayed Wife

Lexicon for Betrayed Wives

Betrayal introduces us to a whole new vocabulary (and I'm not just referring to expletives).

Cake-Eater (see also **Cake-Eater, How to Spot A):** You know, the guy who wants to have his cake and Edith too. A cake-eater is someone with a strong sense of entitlement. He thinks that he deserves a loyal wife at home and a girlfriend (or two) on the side. Cake-eaters are often baffled by the fallout of D-Day because they hadn't really given a whole lot of thought to the consequences of their cheating. You can try to reconcile with a cake-eater, but unless he has a serious reckoning with his own assholery, you're likely in for a whole lot more heartbreak.

Exit Affair: There are those (mostly women) who use an affair as a way to get out of a marriage. It's a method for cowards who instead of owning up to their desire to leave the marriage, force the hand of their partner to essentially kick them out. This absolves them from being the one who left the marriage. Instead of "I asked for a divorce," the narrative becomes "she kicked me out." The partner gets cast as the enemy rather than the victim.

Other Woman (see also **Open Letter to the Other Woman):** ie. Not the "woman" who's the wife. The other one. Who's not supposed to be in the marriage.

Fence-Sitter: Ah yes, the fence-sitter. The guy who just doesn't know what he wants. The guy who "loves you but is not in love with you." The guy who just wants you to be patient with him while he continues to see his girlfriend but still enjoys all the benefits of marriage/family. The guy who just can't decide. A fence-sitter will sit on that bloody fence as long as you'll let him, whining about how *confusing* this all is.

Pick-me dance: Ugh. So many of us do this to ourselves. We learn of a partner's affair and go into some sort of self-humiliation in which we try to remake ourselves into the perfect partner for our cheating spouse. We become a sex goddess, a fashion icon, a perfect 50s housewife. We don't trouble him with our pain. Oh no! We stuff down our distress, we bat our eyelashes as we soak up every bit of his bullshit, and desperately hope that he picks us. The prize? Well, not much really. A guy who cheated on us and who isn't being held accountable for it. If you're doing the pick-me dance, I urge you to learn some new steps. Steps that take you right to the office of your lawyer or your therapist. Or both.

Lies We Believe After His Affair

It's hard to overstate how much being cheated on messes with our heads. But sometimes we do the most damage to ourselves. In the wake of betrayal, we tell ourselves all sorts of untruths, based on a deep fear and a conviction that, if we've been betrayed by someone we trusted, there must be something wrong with us.

Not all of us do this, of course. Those among us with healthy self-esteem often go straight to outrage. A marriage counsellor said that he didn't worry about the women who got angry. He worried about the ones who didn't. They, he said, were the ones more likely to blame themselves.

Blaming ourselves can be strangely appealing. If it was somehow our fault, we reason (fallaciously), that if we fix ourselves, our spouse won't cheat again.

Uh...no.

It doesn't help, of course, that our culture piles on. If a guy cheats, it's because his wife was frigid. Frumpy. A nag. On some level, a lot of us believe those lies, even when our husbands are swearing that's not it at all. Harder still, of course, is when our husbands join in, blaming us for their choice to cheat.

Before long, the chorus of lies reaches a crescendo, making the truth almost impossible to hear.

With that in mind, I've compiled a list of the lies...along with the truth. Which, a wise soul has said, will set us free.

1. **The lie: "I'm a fool."**

I hear this one a lot. "I'm such a fool for believing he loved me." "I'm a total fool for thinking he'd never cheat." "He made a fool of me."

The truth: You're a loyal wife and friend who trusted someone who betrayed that trust.

2. **The lie: "I'll never get past this."**

The truth: Yes, you will. It will take time. Far longer than you would expect (experts generally say three to five years...I was closer to five). But within that time, you'll inch your way closer to a better marriage (if you choose to stay) or a better life (if you choose to go). You'll work through the pain and get to a place where you recognize that this wasn't about you. You were collateral damage. You'll get past it to a place where being betrayed is something that happened.

3. **The lie: "He cheated because she must be amazing in bed."**

The truth: He cheated because he was seeking something outside himself that's missing inside himself. He cheated because he liked the reflection of himself he saw in her eyes. He cheated because it felt exciting and dangerous. He cheated because he was able to convince himself that it was somehow okay. That he deserved it. That nobody would get hurt. He cheated because he's capable of self-delusion. He cheated because he has addiction issues. The list, sadly, goes on.

4. **The lie: "She must have had something I didn't."**

The truth: What she had, you don't want. Being an Other Woman is rarely like in the movies. While there might be champagne and roses (at least at the start), there's also cancelled rendezvous, erectile dysfunction, arguments, lonely nights and holidays...and a future that's more about promises than plans. What's more, to participate as an OW, you need to convince yourself that you somehow have more claim on this guy than the person whom he promised to love, honour and cherish. That life (or his wife) is complicating your future together, not him. That all that stuff he says to you is true, even though you know that, at some point, he said the same stuff to his wife. That lying about you and hiding you away is evidence of his love. You want that? Didn't think so.

5. **The lie: "He cheated because I gained weight/got pregnant/got depressed/got sick..."**

The truth: He cheated because he wasn't emotionally equipped to deal with his own issues. He cheated to escape. Any guy who cheats because his wife gains weight, gets pregnant, is dealing with a disabled child or an aging parent or whatever is a total dick who needs to be shown the door anyway. Any guy who cheats is, frankly, someone incapable of having a healthy relationship, one that includes really tough conversations. Marriage has a steep learning curve. Few of us saw healthy marriages played out for us. It's hard to know how to broach tough topics, like waning attraction due to weight gain or pregnancy, fear of fatherhood, feelings of abandonment. Many of us don't even really know what we're feeling...we just know we're feeling lonely and misunderstood. An affair can seem appealing. But the smart ones among us recognize that's a dangerous path to go down. That it will cause more problems than it will solve. They're the ones who give their marriage a fighting chance before they blow it up. The others...well...we know what happens.

6. **The lie: "My happiness depends on him."**

The truth: Your happiness depends on you. It always did. Too many of us have bought into pop-song wisdom about finding our soulmates and living happily ever after. Happy comes, generally, after enough soul searching that we have exorcised our own demons and discover a deep sense of worth in ourselves, no matter what the world says about us.

7. **The lie: "My marriage will never the same (it will be worse)."**

The truth: My marriage will never be the same (it can be better). I would have called total bullshit on that a few years ago. I would have scoffed, of course it can be better if he's not sleeping with other people. But really good? Nah. But here I am, eating my words. Rebuilding a marriage takes a lot of work. It takes a deep commitment on the part of your husband to recognize how badly he's hurt you and how he's damaged your relationship. And it takes a strong desire to want to be a better person. To deserve your love and trust. And you've got some work to do too. To take a good look at your marriage and take responsibility for your own shortcomings. (This is in no way to say you were to blame for his cheating. That's on him. But there isn't a marriage in the world in which just one partner is to blame for issues within it.) And then, slowly, you rebuild. A few years later, you just might be amazed at how strong that marriage feels. And how deep the love goes.

That's the truth.

M

Marital Therapy (See also Couples Counsellor, How to Find A Good)

Hiking Girl, one of our Club members, shared this about her marital therapy:

My marriage would not have survived without getting the help we needed. We started therapy one week after D-Day. Around three months after D-Day, I was sitting in therapy and I had hit a wall, I just said 'I'm stuck I don't see how I will ever forgive and move on. I don't want to live my life like this.' I was ready for a divorce. I had asked him all the questions that I needed answers to, and since I had no more questions, I stopped showing him my emotions. I was starting to feel like it was this big elephant in the room and we were sweeping it under the carpet. Our therapist gave us this to work on:

1. See emotion as opportunity to connect.

2. Identify the emotion.

3. Understand it from your wife's perspective.

4. Apologize/"what can I do to help you?"

She told my husband to think of an Oreo cookie. He was scratching at the cookie part when what he needed to do was dig deep into the creamy center and have empathy and really feel my pain. She told him if you don't do this, she will never get over this. She was so right. I started talking to him when I was having a bad day or if I was getting a trigger. I woke him up in the middle of the night to hold me after a nightmare. I shared my mind movies. I no longer cried alone in the bathroom. I cried in front of him whenever I needed to. I let him see the raw pain I was in. I'm 22 months now, and I will always be very open with my emotions. We are in a much better place, he has changed so many things about himself and our marriage is so much stronger then it was before the affair.

MEDITATION/MINDFULNESS

I often dread it, this sitting on my cushion for 10 minutes that feels like hours. Realizing my foot is itchy, my hip aches. Realizing I forgot to take something out of the freezer to thaw for dinner. That I still need to send that email, fill out that permission form for school, buy my friend a birthday gift. It's called the Monkey Mind, that constant chatter in our heads.

But beyond the chatter is that small voice, the one that often speaks wisdom we've long forgotten. It's a voice that holds our truth and, for me at least, it requires sitting still, labelling that chatter as "thoughts" as they drift along my consciousness, and being patient (being so bloody patient!) until I can access what's deeper. Sometimes what's deeper is a sadness I've been keeping at bay. Sometimes, it's a fear I haven't wanted to acknowledge. Or a vulnerability that has disguised itself as cynicism or jadedness. Sometimes it's boredom. But it's always something that has been lurking in the shadows, waiting to be called out into the light.

Plenty of us will do almost anything to avoid being alone with our thoughts. A recent study asked participants to sit for 10 minutes alone in an empty room. If they wanted to be released, they could administer an electric shock to themselves. Most chose the shock over the emptiness. As Anne Lamott puts it, "My mind is like a bad neighbourhood. I try not to go there alone."

But it has been through sitting with those uncomfortable feelings as they arose that has stripped them of their power over me. By holding them, I have realized they will not swallow me, that, like a wave, they will crest and recede, sometimes not as quickly as I'd like. But always losing some strength as they go.

You can heal from betrayal without meditating. But I wish everyone would try it, because it will heal you in places you might not even know you're wounded. It will strengthen you from the inside out.

Try this Tonglen meditation ("Tonglen" is Tibetan for sending and taking):

Take your seat on the floor or on a chair. Sit straight up, as if you're rooted below but extending your head toward the sky.

Breathe. In. Out.

As you take a deep breath in, take in suffering. Your own. Others'. The world's.

As you slowly exhale, send out compassion. For yourself. For others. For the world.

I promise you, with time, these breaths will heal you.

Mind Movies

I hated turning out the light. Whether awake or asleep, my mind would feature graphic, disturbing and totally invented movies of my husband's affair. It was relentless, an endless loop of images that rendered me incapable of doing little more than whimpering.

It wasn't just at night, though. Sometimes they'd hit in the middle of the day. They'd often feature sex but sometimes also clichéd romantic scenes. Candlelight dinners, gift-giving, hand-holding, laughing. Anything that cast them as romantic leads and me as the discarded has-been, the nobody, the fool.

Thing is, nobody, not even porn stars, could have the type of passionate, agile, constant sex that I imagined. And this wasn't my husband subjecting me to these images, it was me hurting myself. It was mental self-flagellation. It felt like my dirty secret.

I finally confessed to my therapist, who suggested some strategies to clip the mind movies quickly. It didn't work every time but, with practice, they faded away. Here's what she suggested:

"Stop"

Imagine a huge red stop sign every time your mind starts to go down the path that ends with whatever particularly fetid fantasy you have. If you can, give yourself a stern out-loud "Stop!"

Snap

Put an elastic band around your wrist and give it a good snap whenever you imagine things that damage your psyche. Your brain will associate the fantasizing with the pain of the elastic snapping your skin and cut the mind movie short.

Replace

Constantly focusing on the "other" – spouse, other woman, whatever – disempowers you. One thing that worked for me was replacing my mental sex tapes with mind movies of a different sort, starring me. In some versions, I was behind the wheel of my car chasing the OW naked down the road. I imagined the fear on her face. I imagined her butt jiggling in a distinctly UN-sexy way. It always ended up making me giggle.

If you're a better person than I and can't fathom imagining inflicting pain and/or humiliation on the OW, try a mind movie of you doing something that makes you feel good: Winning an award, running a race, hanging with your kids. Anything that replaces painful images with positive ones.

Lynn Less Pain from the BWC has her version of stopping mind movies: *Sometimes it just sucks. Yell 'fuck it' into an empty room. In the next room, say a prayer. You just get by every day but it lessens with time. Most of the time, I thought about sticking a porcupine up both their asses.*

My Heartbreak, My Rules

There's a saying in Betrayed Wives Club, courtesy of member Steam: *My heartbreak, my rules. "If your husband wants you to even consider giving him a second chance, then he needs to make it crystal clear to you that he deserves it. How? By acquiescing to what you need to feel safe. My heartbreak, my rules."*

What that means is this:

1. Total transparency: Sure he could have a burner phone hidden beneath the front seat of his car. But that doesn't mean you shouldn't still insist on access to any and all modes of communication: phones, passwords, email addresses, cell bills.
2. Total accountability: Is he where he says he is? Is he with the person he says he's with? Is he doing what he says he's doing? Can he provide evidence for any/all of his claims? This isn't about surveillance on your part. It's about him earning back trust, day by day, week by week, by showing that his word means something.
3. Total honesty: He needs to answer every single question you have with the truth. Not a version of the truth. Not a sliver of truth. The whole truth. Whatever it is you want to know.

4. Total commitment: He needs to be all-in if you're going to rebuild your marriage. If he's on the fence about you, if he's still offering up the "I just can't choose. I think I love both of you," if he's delivering the "I love you but I don't think I'm in love with you" bullshit, then he's not fully committed to rebuilding your marriage. Which means, if you're going to stay with this ding-dong, you're going to be doing all the heavy lifting. Forget it. You're exhausted enough.

N

Nature

I am an admitted tree-hugger, but there's science to back up my conviction that nature heals. Even just viewing pictures of nature has been shown to reduce anger, aggression and anxiety. What's more, it ups our "awe," which is our sense that the world is so much bigger than we are but that we are an integral part of a beautiful whole. Best of all, nature is free. So here's my prescription for a broken heart: Embrace nature. Go for a walk in the woods or a city park, making sure to breathe in the magic healing powers (seriously!) of the mighty trees. If you're near water, close your eyes and just listen to the sounds. Listen to birds. Stare at the sky (see also **Cloud Appreciation Society**). Place a vase of bright tulips on your kitchen table. Google nature photos on your laptop.

Narcissistic Personality Disorder

•Inflated sense of own importance.

•Deep need for excessive attention and admiration.

•Expect credit for being "special" even in absence of any accomplishments.

•Troubled relationships.

•Lack of empathy for others.

•Fragile self-esteem.

•Inability to hear criticism.

•Difficulty regulating emotions.

Narcissists are almost textbook cheaters, which is why so much of our culture's narrative around cheating is black-and-white. Thing is, while a lot of narcissists are cheaters, not all cheaters are narcissists.

Nonetheless, if the cheater in your life checks off most of the boxes for NPD, you're smart to pack up and get out. People with NPD are resistant to treatment. They're not the problem, their thinking goes. It's everybody else.

They're wrong. It's not you. It's them. Save yourself.

Next Right Step

Glennon Doyle, author of "Love Warrior," has said that our feelings, which so many of us spend considerable time and effort trying to avoid, are simply guides. They are our personal prophets pointing the way toward the next right thing.

The *next* right step. Let me explain.

Many of us, post D-Day, spend the next weeks and months mentally spinning in terror because we're faced with a HUGE decision. Do we stay and rebuild our marriage? Or leave and rebuild a life without him? I spent about two years in that suspended state of fear. Stay or go? My hand constantly on the door handle. My bags metaphorically packed. "One wrong move, buddy..." could have been my motto.

Of course, underscoring that BIG QUESTION is the deeper fear: *Will my heart be broken again?*

When betrayed wives lay out their story and ask me whether I think they should stay, they might be hoping I'll trot out the statistics about re-offending (1 in 5 or 1 in 2, depending on who you ask). They might believe I have some deep intel into the mindset of the average cheater. But more likely, they're looking desperately for reassurance that they're safe now. That they won't ever EVER have to go through such hell again.

Because, man oh man, those feelings were *excruciating*.

I wish I could offer that reassurance.

I wish I could guarantee that every guy who cheats works tirelessly to become a man who deserves that second (or sometimes third) chance.

Some guys do exactly that, of course, and their marriages become stronger and richer as a result. But we all also know that many do not. That many squander that second (or third) chance and break their wives' hearts all over again.

In the absence of a crystal ball, you need to pay attention to those feelings, those personal prophets.

They can't predict THE right thing to do, but they can guide you toward the NEXT right thing.

There's more than one next right step, of course. Your next right step might be to sit down with a lawyer to better understand what a separation might look like or what your finances might allow. Your next right step might be booking a weekly massage to give you the space to simply feel nurtured. It might be a getaway with a compassionate girlfriend. It might be finding a babysitter so that you can get out for a run or drive somewhere in your car to scream regularly or get yourself as quickly as possible to your 12-step group so that you don't fall off the wagon.

What your next right step is NOT is anything that harms

you, body or soul. Your next right step is NOT to sleep with your husband's brother for revenge. It is NOT to drink or shop or gamble to excess. The purpose of your next right step is to take care of yourself, to learn how to sit with your own pain and trust that you are strong enough to withstand it. Your next right step teaches you that you don't have to know how this is going to turn out. It reminds us that none of us ever knows how our life is going to turn out. That is an illusion that most of us live under until we're blindsided by the news that our husbands were not who we thought they were and our marriages were not what we thought they were.

Living this way eliminates any possibility of falling down that rabbit hole in which you're already rehearsing the conversation you'll have with your daughter on her wedding day (though right now she's in preschool) about how sorry you are that you made such a mess of your own marriage. It eliminates the paralysis that comes with trying to make decisions that you're simply not ready to make. Whether or not to end the marriage? Maybe that's your NEXT right thing...but maybe you just need to separate. Or sleep in separate bedrooms. Or take a weekend holiday together.

It's a mindset that extends beyond infidelity. It gives us permission to not be entirely sure where we're going. To feel safe only thinking one step ahead. Next right step. You can walk the whole path to healing that way.

No

"No" is a complete sentence.

O

Open Letter to the Other Woman

Dear OW,

WTF?

Honestly, just what the fuck were you thinking? You *knew* he was married. You *knew* he had children. You *knew* he slept beside me every night. And you knew that *I* knew nothing. Is that what made it so delicious? So tempting? That I appeared by his side at various events, clueless to what was going on behind my back? Did you feel triumphant? That you'd beat me at something?

Okay, I looked stupid, at least to you. Is the satisfaction of that worth sacrificing your own dignity? Because, really, how can you have any dignity when you're pulling on your panties as he races out the door to be home in time for dinner? How can you have any dignity when you're alone – again – on a Saturday night while he's watching *Toy Story* with his children and tucking them into bed?

And frankly, though I might have looked stupid and pitiful to you and some less-than-compassionate others, I'll take stupid over sleazy and low and cruel any day of the week.

No matter how awful it felt to be me when I found out, I'd still take that over being you. No matter that my eyes were practically swollen shut from crying, I could still look myself in the mirror without shame.

Did you think it was a matter of time? That he would walk away from the life we'd built? That those fantasies you'd convinced yourself of – I nagged, I was lousy in bed, I was boring and bitchy – were true? Did you really believe that any relationship based on deception would deliver you from your unhappiness?

My guess is, yes, you did. My guess is that very few Other Women honestly admit their role as an accomplice in the intentional hurting and deception of another human being, often another human being they don't know. Or barely know. Or perhaps, shockingly, know well. Instead, they sell themselves clichés. "We're soulmates," "we couldn't help ourselves," "the chemistry was too powerful" or "you can't stop love." All of which, I suspect you recognize on some level, is total bullshit. All of which allows you to divorce your abhorrent actions from your intent. "We didn't mean to hurt anyone," you wail.

Oh. Yes. You. Did.

Because you knew. You knew that I was being hurt, even if *I* didn't yet know it. You knew I was being lied to. Betrayed. And you participated in that. Knowingly. Willingly. Perhaps even happily.

What's more, my children were being hurt. And though I don't expect you to take total responsibility for that (after all, HE was their father), you nonetheless contributed to the potential dissolution of their family.

And for what?

Was the sex that good? Were the feelings of superiority, if only for the brief time he was with you, so intoxicating that it made all the humiliating departures, all the embarrassment when you were caught, all the shame this no doubt triggered, worth it?

And if he left me for you? What would you have gained? Three emotionally wrung out children every second weekend. A man who lies and cheats. A man who doesn't have the self-control to stop himself from doing something he knows to be wrong and hurtful. What a prize. Guess what? If he's not willing to become something better than that – he's all yours. At least until he meets another you in the future and you're cast as the betrayed wife.

You were shocked when he, caught and given the choice between me or you, didn't hesitate. Not for a second. Believe it or not, I felt sorry for you. Though I raged at you in my head, loathed the look of you, wanted to spit each time I said your name and shower each time I imagined you two together, I nonetheless felt a sliver of pity for you. Because no one does this unless they value themselves so little that they settle for another's scraps rather than demand respect. Or unless they're so delusional that they really believe that this is how true love manifests. Unless they've fallen for all that "star-crossed lovers" and "us against the world" crap.

It has been years. I have no idea where you are now. And though I occasionally taste anger when I think back, I'm able to wish you, if not well, then at least better than what you had. If only to spare another woman the agony of finding out that you're sleeping with her husband.

Signed,

Elle

180, The

If you've gone online at all seeking support after discovering a husband's affair, you've likely read about The 180. It's credited to Michele Weiner Davis, author of "Divorce Busting" (which I haven't read), and it's an overwhelming 33 points long. The 180 can be an effective strategy to protect yourself if you're still with a partner who you suspect is cheating but he's denying it, or who won't end the affair, or who is giving you that old cheaters' chestnut, "I just can't *decide*." Though I think that any guy who won't end an affair IMMEDIATELY should be shown the door, I understand how some of us can't make the decision right away for any number of reasons. Which is where The 180 comes in. The point of it is to remove yourself as much as possible from the marriage while remaining in it – a sort of Shrödinger's cat of post-betrayal matrimony. So, though you're sharing a roof, you're no longer acting as a wife. You don't cook his meals, you don't wash his clothes, you don't call to check up on where he is, you don't insist he sit down and listen to you outline why he should pick you. You do make an appointment with a lawyer, you do everything you can to heal yourself. The main goal is to help you begin to move forward in your life. But you are also creating a situation in which he's getting a taste of life without you, which might have the consequence of helping him pull his head out of his ass.

There are parts of The 180 that I don't support. Parts that feel regressive and manipulative. And I think 33 rules can be daunting to someone who's just been betrayed and can't remember her own middle name, let alone what #19 is of The 180 is. So I've created an abbreviated version of The 180. Let's call it The BWCredo:

1. Don't try to sell him on the marriage or you. You are not a Tinder profile.

2. Set clear boundaries (see also **Boundaries**) and enforce them.

3. Don't enlist his family or friends to convince him to see your value.

4. Don't schedule dates together. As long as the OW is in his life, that's one woman too many for this relationship.

5. Do *more* than act as if you are moving on with your life; begin moving on with your life! This is about radical self-care. Massage. Pedicure. Good books. A concert. Coffee with friends. Whatever fills you up.

6. Don't discuss the marriage until he is ready to provide full disclosure to you regarding the affair, re-commit to your marriage and actively taking steps to seek help for himself.

7. Avoid responding when he tries to provoke you. Give yourself a time out. Go for a walk. Count to 100 in your head. No one ever got themselves into trouble by just not saying anything.

8. Promises are not enough. You need to see action from him.

9. Act with self-respect, integrity and honesty. Don't change who you are for anybody, least of all someone who has cheated on you.

Other Woman (OW)

The Other Woman holds a certain allure in our cultural mythology, doesn't she? She's sexy as hell, right? Short skirt. Revealing top. Long hair. Long legs. She has a husky cigarettes-and-whiskey voice. Come-hither eyes.

It's fiction. A total fantasy. Sure, some Other Women are attractive. But the vast majority look like the checkout clerk at your grocery store. They look like your son's third grade teacher. They look like your hair stylist, or your dentist. They look like, well, they look like anybody. Because here's the thing: Other Women aren't Other Women because they are impossible to resist. They are Other Women because they lack a moral code that says "do not sleep with married men." (I'm excluding those "accidental" Other Women who honestly think this guy chatting them up at the bar is single.

And who, when they discover otherwise, tell him to take a hike, send an anonymous message to his wife if possible, and vow to vet potential dates more intensely.) They are Other Women not because of what they look like, or their sexual gymnastics, or their worldly accomplishments, they're Other Women because they lack boundaries. Because they're willing to settle for runner-up status. Because they have convinced themselves that they can live with this because they believe it's temporary. Sometimes they're Other Women because they're sad and manipulative and desperate.

Unfortunately, that's appealing to a guy in search of someone to prop up his pathetic ego. Someone who, when he looks into her eyes doesn't see her but rather sees a new-and-improved version of himself reflected back – more interesting, sexier, funnier, more successful. That is the appeal of the Other Woman. Not her, necessarily, but what she represents. An escape from the monotony of life. A reprieve from feelings of inadequacy or boredom or loneliness or stress or fear. The affair is a fantasy.

And our lack of understanding of what an affair really is leads so many of us, when we find out our husbands are cheating, to respond with: *Seriously? With her? What the hell??*

But, sometimes, they're gorgeous. It's like they walked out of Central Casting on their long, slim legs. And it can feel like a knockout blow to our self-esteem. I'm reminded of what my husband's counsellor said to me: "What these women have is nothing you want." Their skin might be flawless but their morals aren't. We all know a beautiful someone who grew uglier the more we recognized just how vacuous and/or morally repugnant she was. Relegate her outside the margins of your life. Do what you can to view her as little more than a tumour in your marriage, one that needed removing. And then focus on you. Your healing. Your future. Free of toxic people.

P

Painlympics

Sure it's a made-up word. But it's a good one that perfectly sums up our tendency to want to out-suffer our spouse. Especially when our spouse implies that his behaviour was the consequence of his own suffering. Especially when our stories already include words like abuse and addiction and neglect – when we already survived situations in which we felt powerless over the pain inflicted on us by the people who were supposed to be safeguarding our hearts.

It can feel like another betrayal when so much of the "how to heal from an affair" advice implies that we're somehow responsible, even a teensy bit, for our spouse's affair. It lands like a sucker punch.

It's more infuriating when it's our spouse. Some guy who's ripped out our heart explains that he cheated because he felt neglected when we were nursing our cancer-stricken mother, or tending to our disabled child, or working to pay for our kids' tutor, or going to the gym to get our health under control or maybe just checked out because we were fed up from giving while getting so little in return. Or maybe it was his emotionally absent mother, his abusive father, his drug-addled older brother. He felt lonely. Abandoned. Scared. Unloved.

It's at those moments when we should ensure we don't have access to firearms because Holy Bad Timing.

Thing is he might have a point.

I couldn't hear it at first. I didn't want a whiff of excuse from him. I wanted – and frankly deserved – total accountability from him. Nothing less than "I am so sorry and I will spend the rest of my life trying to be the husband you deserved all along."

But a big part of my inability to hear any explanation for his betrayal of me was my dedication to my own sad-sack story as somehow more deserving of sympathy than his.

I honestly believed that if there was a painlympics – a contest in which the suffering I'd endured was measured against his – that I would go home with the Gold. He'd be lucky to make the podium.

What's more, I felt I deserved a medal for having conquered those demons. Sure my childhood sucked, but I'd spent much of my adulthood trying to learn the right stuff and shake off the wrong stuff.

Besides, I figured I'd had my quota of pain. The universe owed me an easy time of it. I'd made peace with my addict mother. I'd dumped (or been dumped by) the bad boyfriends and married the nice guy. I was healed. Cue the hallelujahs.

Turns out, not so much healed as *healing*.

It also turns out that the universe isn't keeping score.

But when we engage in the painlympics – measuring our own pain against others' in order to determine who's more entitled to victimhood – nobody wins.

I learned this the hard way.

Case in point: A few years ago my daughter was disappointed that she didn't get the part she wanted in a play. She really wanted it. She worked hard for it. "It's not fair," she wailed. "I never get picked," she cried.

I was empathetic, at least at first. I understood her disappointment. I'd *felt*her disappointment. But then I got a bit tired of it. I tried not to sigh too loudly. I refrained from rolling my eyes. I didn't, however, manage to keep my mouth shut. "There are children who don't have clean water," I pointed out delicately (not for the first time). "There are children sold into bonded slavery." My point was clear: *Your suffering isn't as bad as someone else's so get over yourself.*

Fortunately, I was gifted with a daughter who'll have none of that. With the steely authority of a prosecutor, she admitted that, yes, she knows other children have it worse. But, she said, right now she didn't want to hear about them. Right now, it was about her. Right now, her pain mattered.

She was right.

Her pain, no matter how small it might measure on some universal scale of suffering, mattered.

So does yours.

So does mine.

So does his.

It all matters.

There is, however, a deeper lesson there. I came to realize that I dismissed my daughter's suffering as somehow less than deserving of my empathy because it made me uncomfortable. I had wanted my daughter to succeed in ways I hadn't. I had wanted to spare her the pain of, well, living in this world. So when it became clear that I was powerless to protect her, I didn't want to hear it. My reaction was akin to covering my ears and insisting that she tell me a better story in which she felt loved and grateful for all her blessings.

But she was wiser than that. Not only did she make it clear that her suffering mattered, she also made it clear that she was strong enough to handle it. More than once in her so-far short life, she's told me, when I play my children that don't have clean water card, that she needs to just be left alone to cry and feel sorry for herself...and that she'll come out of her room when she's feeling better.

And that's exactly what she does.

I've noticed that she's equally capable of being with others in their suffering – no matter how small – without fearing becoming lost in it. She sees it for what it is. An open wound that needs love and compassion to heal.

Suffering doesn't frighten her, it pulls her in.

All suffering matters.

I know this is radical. And I know it pisses off those of us who hold firm to some deep belief in fairness.

People like me, for example. People who inwardly scoff at those whose suffering, in the grand scheme of things, seems pretty silly.

Like a husband who claims that he cheated on us because his mother didn't hug him enough.

Silly, right?

Not exactly.

It took me a few months before I could handle listening to my husband finally purging decades of pain that he'd adeptly buried. But once I did – once I could acknowledge his suffering as no less valid than my own – something shifted. He stopped being the enemy and started being a fellow human being, doing his best (which, frankly, sometimes sucked) to get through.

And that changed everything.

Pain Shopping

There is such a thing as too much information. Some call it "pain shopping" and it's a compulsive need for more and more detail.

I did plenty of pain shopping myself in the weeks following D-Day. My husband would no sooner be out the door than I'd be rooting through his drawers, his suit pockets, his files. Looking for something – anything! – to confirm what I already knew.

And that's the rub. I already knew. What difference did it make if I found yet another restaurant receipt? Or another phone bill detailing the length of the zillion phone calls?

So why was I doing it? I could plead insanity quite convincingly. But, in some weird way, I felt afraid of getting past the betrayal. Not that I was even close – I still had a long way to go. But as I inched closer, a small part of me worried that if I put this behind us, it could sneak up on me again and knock me down. And I wasn't so sure I could survive it again.

And so, on some level, it made sense to keep it in front of me. As long as I was raking my husband over the coals for his affairs, he couldn't possibly think that it wasn't such a big deal. Or that I had handled it fine. There could, quite simply, be absolutely NO mistake that this was NOT okay with me. And would never be okay with me.

The thing is he already knew that. He watched me crumble and it devastated him. He told me once that my eyes looked dead and he knew that he had done that to me.

What the pain shopping was doing was keeping my eyes dead. It was preventing even a glimmer of light from re-entering because the long shadow of the betrayal was still there, casting darkness over everything: my joy in my kids, my delight in my pets, my love of my work.

What's more, you can't un-know something, no matter how painful. After a while (I'm a slow learner!), I came up with my 24-hour rule. If I wanted to ask my husband something about his infidelity, I made myself wait 24 hours (give or take...). If I STILL wanted to know a day later, or could even remember what the question was, I proceeded and he answered honestly.

Usually the question had faded from my mind, indicating to me that it wasn't something I needed to know but rather I was "pain shopping."

To my husband's credit (I do give him some), he recognized that I deserved to decide what information I wanted. But to his counsellor's credit, he sometimes asked me why I wanted to know something, pointing out, gently, that it didn't move us forward but rather compounded the hurt. Sometimes I agreed. Often, I demanded the answer anyway. And it hurt. And it didn't move us forward. The good news is that, many years later, I don't remember a whole lot of what he told me. Kinda like a long-ago movie in which I remember the storyline but not the details.

The story was betrayal. The rest? I've learned not to care.

Perel, Esther (see also "Where Do We Begin")

Esther Perel burst on the infidelity scene a few years ago with her book "Mating In Captivity: Unlocking Erotic Intelligence," in which she argues that monogamy is really hard but that it can be worth the effort it takes to achieve it. Maybe not earth-shattering in its conclusion but backed up by solid research and a refreshing approach. Since then, Perel has made it her mission to reframe our cultural discussions around infidelity. Others have tried, of course (see also **Glass, Shirley**) with some success but Perel benefits from newer tools, including social media, TED Talks and a podcast, that have elevated her to something of a pop star in the world of marital counselling.

Her philosophy around infidelity lines up with my own: It needn't be the deal-breaker that so many of us thought it was and that our culture almost demands. Rather it can be the chance to, as Perel puts it, have a second marriage with your first husband.

But, and it's a big but, her approach can be tough for newly betrayeds to absorb mostly because her compassion extends to the cheating spouse, which can feel infuriating to the betrayed. And though she always holds the cheating spouse accountable, those of us still raw from D-Day, are hungry for blood. We want humiliation for cheaters, not mercy.

Which means Perel might be best left until the shock wears off and our minds open, at least a sliver, to the idea that our cheating partner isn't necessarily a monster but a good person who did a horrible thing.

Polygraph

Perhaps I'd watched too many detective shows over the years but, for a while, I thought insisting my husband take a lie detector test in order to find out whether he was telling me the whole truth was a great idea. As a journalist, however, I do my research. And research revealed that polygraphs are highly unreliable. Rather than measure the truth of a person's response, they measure the physiological arousal of the respondent – his heart rate or perspiration. This means you're getting evidence of the person's feelings about the question as much as his potential answer. In other words, being asked about something you feel guilt and shame about – even if you've already admitted to it – can generate these physiological responses.

You can give it a try, though polygraphs are not cheap. And take note: Enough people Google "how to cheat a polygraph test" that it comes up as a possible search when you simply Google "polygraph".

Porn Addiction

In university, I lived with two guys. It was completely platonic and based on necessity more than desire. I couldn't afford to live alone and, having grown up with a brother, I appreciated the laissez-faire attitude of male roommates.

But every Sunday night, my roommates would go to a nearby video store and rent porn. Really raunchy porn. And though I considered myself open-minded, I loathed the Sunday night porn fest. My bedroom was right above the living room and the sounds (EGADS, the sounds!) would float upward, distracting me from reading, homework or whatever else I was trying to do.

But though I hated it, I nonetheless considered it harmless. And continued to throughout my life.

My husband also thought his secret habit harmless (though I've come to understand that anything we feel the need to keep secret is often our first clue that, on some level, we know we shouldn't be doing it). It wasn't until after D-Day that he confessed the extent of his porn habit. And it wasn't until he really examined what messages he got from porn (that women were always sexually available, that all women want it fast and furious, that women are objects to satisfy men) that he could acknowledge just how far along the path to porn addiction he'd ventured.

Do I think all porn is bad? No, I do not.

I think much of it degrades women, but not all. I think, like anything that removes us from our lives and offers an intoxicating tonic of entitlement and easy access, porn can be dangerous.

Brené Brown tells us why porn can be particularly appealing. A therapist she spoke with for her book "Daring Greatly" commented about the shame men experience around actual or anticipated sexual rejection, and the vulnerability men feel in the sexual arena. Enter porn, he said. "For five bucks and five minutes, you think you're getting what you need, and *you don't have to risk rejection*."

Brown called the comment "revelatory" for her because, like so many women, she'd always assumed that porn was about men seeking novelty, sexual expertise, spectacular bodies. Of course porn provides that. But in this therapist's point of view, the appeal of porn is that there's no rejection. "The secret is that sex is terrifying for most men," he said, noting that porn offers "power and control." (Hardly makes porn harmless; there's still evidence that viewing it alters neural pathways in the brain.)

My husband said the same for years but I didn't believe him. Or rather, I listened and then dismissed what he'd told me in favor of self-bashing. My body isn't firm enough. My breasts are too small. My sexual gymnastics aren't exciting enough. My husband's insisted that porn never provided what he now understands he craved – intimacy.

The rest of us assume, because sex is generally fun, that, as addictions go, one that allows you to indulge in sex anywhere with anyone has to be a laugh-riot. Or that watching it is harmless fun.

It's not. It's steeped in the same shame and fear of other addictions, no matter what mask it's wearing.

Post-Infidelity Stress Disorder (see Trauma)

Yes, this is an actual thing that more therapists recognize. PISD is PTSD. It is awful. And it is treatable.

Power, Your

We have the power to decide what it is that we will tolerate in our marriage after betrayal. We have power to carefully consider the consequences of a partner's deception, or continuing deception after we've agreed to give them a second chance.

We can make calculations, perhaps with the help of a therapist who's more clear-eyed than we are. We can determine what we want the rest of our life to look like if our partner cannot or will not become someone who deserves a second chance. And we get to decide what that looks like. We get to determine what our second chance consists of. Do we insist they get therapy? Do we insist that they attend a 12-step group? Do we insist upon treatment for their depression/addiction/anxiety/ADHD/impulse control/whatever? Do we insist that they steer clear of "friends" who enabled the cheating? As BWC member Steam puts it so perfectly, "My heartbreak, my rules."

It won't be easy. The right decision isn't always the easy one, though a lot of us also buy into the delusion that if it's the right decision, it will "feel" right. Nope. Not if we're accustomed to a lifetime (or even a few years) of not paying attention to our instincts. It takes practice to trust ourselves. It's a muscle that needs developing.

But that, my fierce soul-warriors, is where your power rests. In the knowledge that you have what it takes to keep yourself safe. In the recognition that you control you and nobody else.

Prostitutes, When He Cheats With

If there is a ranking in cheating, "prostitutes" might be the "best" or the "worst," depending on your point of view. There's rarely an emotional connection, which can make the betrayal less complicated. It's "just sex," according to the guys who do it. And some women, at least on my site, agree. Others, however, feel a betrayal related also to the amount of money secretly spent. What's more, it's usually the lying more than the actual sex that is the most painful aspect of betrayal for betrayed partners to recover from, and not telling your partner you've been with a prostitute definitely falls under "lying by omission."

The difference, sometimes, with prostitutes is that it offers no-strings-attached sex for those with sexual addiction (see also **Sex Addiction**/see also **Carnes, Patrick**) or the chance to explore sexually deviant (I use the term clinically, not pejoratively) behaviour, safe from judgement. What's more, prostitutes won't reject men, so it can feel emotionally safe to someone with intimacy or self-esteem issues.

Ultimately, however, cheating is cheating is cheating.

PRIVACY

Betrayed Wife: [Checks husband's text messages.]

Husband: "But that's a violation of my privacy."

Betrayed Wife: "Yes. It is. But you used your 'privacy' to take a wrecking ball to my heart. Your 'privacy' cannot be worth more to you than this marriage. If it is, please tell me now."

H: "You're treating me like a child."

W: "You violated my trust and I want to give you the chance to step up to repair that breach. What that means is that you have freedom to do what you want but I will verify that you are where/with who/doing what you say you are. This how trust is rebuilt."

H: "I can't believe you don't trust me."

W: "Yeah. It's a real shocker, isn't it? But when you show me that you can't be trusted, then, yeah, I'm not gonna trust you until you show me something different."

Q

❧

Questions

If you're like me, you have badgered your husband with questions: *Who was she? Where did you meet? What does she look like? Did you talk about me? Did she know about me? How many times did you have sex? What type of sex? Where? What type of underpants did she wear? Did you take her to dinner? What did she order?* And on. And on. And on.

My husband answered, mostly. And I think it's important that he did. As Shirley Glass (see also **Glass, Shirley**), who wrote the iconic infidelity guide "Not Just Friends" puts it: "In a love affair, the unfaithful partner has built a wall to shut out the marriage partner and has opened a window to let in the affair partner. To re-establish a marriage that is intimate and trusting after an affair, the walls and the windows must be reconstructed to conform to the safety code and keep the structure of the marriage so that it can withstand the test of time. You install a picture window between you and your marriage partner and construct a solid or opaque wall to block out contact with the affair partner. This arrangement of walls and windows nurtures your marriage and protects it from outside elements and interference."

To clarify Glass's homebuilding metaphor, the marriage needs transparency. The window must be open to the betrayed wife so that she can see exactly what this affair looked like. Blind trust is gone. Mature trust – trust that is earned through your spouse's words matching up with his actions – can grow. But not until you get the answers you need and he starts giving them to you.

The thing is, cheaters feel lousy, unless they're psychopaths or narcissists (see also **Narcissistic Personality Disorder**). They know what they did was hurtful and selfish. And by giving you the details of that, they're forced to acknowledge that not only to you (who, ummm, already knows) but to themselves. It's a lot easier to stay mum, and pretend it's because they don't want to hurt *you*. They already have! But to face that hurt in your eyes again and again feels crappy. Hence the litany of excuses:

"We need to move on and stop rehashing the past."

"You're keeping us stuck."

"Ummm...I don't remember. And it really didn't matter anyway."

There is a danger, however, of something we refer to as pain shopping (see also **Pain Shopping**). It's worth considering what you're asking and what difference it will make to know.

Nonetheless, I don't know of any couples who have successfully rebuilt their marriage without this brutally painful step. During a partner's affair, the door is shut to us. It's time to open the windows and let us see what it was like, while firmly shutting the door to the affair partner.

R

Rebuilding a Marriage

If there's something consistent among betrayed wives who rebuild strong marriages, it's this: they draw clear lines, state their demands and insist upon accountability. They understand that giving someone a second chance is a gift. And that they get to decide whether their partners deserve that second chance. They look with critical eyes at what, exactly, their partner is doing to create the conditions for reconciliation. And they don't compromise.

From the outside, it almost looks easy, as though some people know the rules better than the rest of us. That they have access to a post-betrayal roadmap that the rest of us don't have.

And maybe they do. Maybe that post-betrayal roadmap is something they've had all along. But it amounts to this: We are worthy of respect and dignity and honesty. And it's from that place of knowingness, that place of valuing ourselves that we must respond to a partner's betrayal.

For the rest of us, those who aren't rooted in this belief that we matter, it will be tough. We will doubt. We will wonder what's wrong with us that made our partners cheat. We may slip into self-blame. But we must pull ourselves away from that and remember: We are worthy. We are and have always been enough and if our partners can't remember that too, then there's the door.

Try to imagine responding from that place. Imagine being a person who believes herself worthy. How would you respond differently? Would you be able to calmly make demands? Would you be able to make it clear that you have rules for reconciliation that he can either follow or leave? Would you be able to better feel the pain and the fear without losing yourself in it?

What I'm suggesting is difficult for so many of us. But that difficulty comes from who we believe ourselves to be in the world. It comes from valuing another's love for us over our ability to love ourselves, and that will always create a power imbalance in a marriage. It comes from fear that if we don't make it easy to love us, then we won't be loved.

But if your partner is asking for a second chance, then here's the deal. Lay it out. Creating conditions to rebuild a marriage isn't about punishing him. It's about creating a safe space in which you can establish trust and a marriage based on honesty. It's about loving yourself at least as much as you love the other person.

It's about healing yourself through dignity and self-respect. No matter the outcome of your marriage, you will be loved if you're able to love yourself.

Reconciliation Contract

Years ago on a talk radio program, a caller asked an on-air psychologist whether she should give her husband a second chance after discovering an affair. The psychologist suggested a "reconciliation contract," which, in that particular case, involved the husband agreeing to give the wife his boat if he were to cheat again. I could just imagine this guy, tears on his cheeks, watching his wife drive away, pulling his boat on a trailer behind. All because this guy couldn't keep it in his pants. And if he didn't cheat again? Then great. They could cruise into their future together.

I did not do this. For one thing, my husband doesn't have a boat. For another, it was all I could do to string words together to form a sentence post D-Day. Creating a contract (except, perhaps, contracting a killer to put a hit on my husband) was beyond my capabilities.

I don't know of anyone who's done this, but that doesn't mean it's not still a good idea. It just means it's a good idea that I have yet to see put into practice. If you have, or know someone who did, please share the details.

Repeat Offenders

What if he does it again? And why wouldn't he? we think. *After all, he got away with it this time.*

Snowbird, one of our Betrayed Wives Club members, says this:

To those dealing with repeat offenders, I told my husband this: If you can't control your behavior, we might be friends but we won't be married. Therapy, medication and meetings were game-changers for him. Sixteen months and counting.

I hear often about repeat offenders. Guys who never broke it off, guys who reconnected with the OW, guys who began an affair with another OW. It can feel even worse. *Fool me once...*

But giving someone a second chance doesn't make you a fool. Have your conditions for reconciliation in place. Make your boundaries clear. Be equally clear about the consequences of violating those. Write it all down so if you're reeling from another D-Day, you can follow your own plan.

Rest

We are a culture of do-ers. We think that action is the same as progress. We think that taking our time to figure out what we want now, given this new and devastating information, is wimpy. That unless we respond with holy hell, we're doormats. But let me weigh in with a resounding ***hell no***! Sitting with this new information, assessing your husband's ability and/or desire to recommit to his marriage, and letting your body absorb the shock can be a smart and sane response. Don't let anyone or anything force you to respond in any way inconsistent with what you're ready for, whether that is kick him out or forgive him.

There are times, of course, when you have no choice. A husband who leaves, for instance, isn't giving you much input into whether or not you stay married. Statistically, however, most guys who cheat don't want to lose their marriage (we'll ignore, for the moment, just how fucked up that is) so, likely, you're the one who feels forced to make a choice.

But doing nothing right now, other than figuring out your next right step (see also **Next Right Step**), is perfectly okay. Rest.

Re-trauma (See also Trauma)

Over the 10 years I've maintained Betrayed Wives Club, it's clear that some of us are harder hit by infidelity than others.

That's not to say any of us get off easy. Infidelity is excruciating. It is to say, however, that some of us are devastated. And others of us are absolutely crippled by it.

For those of us who brought certain wounds into our marriage, infidelity re-opens those wounds. In my case, having grown up with alcoholic parents in an emotionally unsafe home, marriage (specifically to my husband) became my safe place. I believed that I'd created a safe zone with a safe person in a highly unsafe world. I let my guard down. *Whew*.

And then...

Pow.

The guy I thought *had* my back was cheating *behind* my back. And all those feelings I thought had been exorcised – my anxiety, my shame, my fear of abandonment, my deep, deep hurt from all those broken promises – came back with a vengeance. I couldn't trust anyone, I deduced. But underneath it all was that childhood conviction that I wasn't worth loving. I wasn't enough.

Turns out my working theory is supported by some pretty smart people. "Not Just Friends" author Shirley Glass has this to say about it:

"Individuals who did not develop basic trust during childhood are especially vulnerable to deception by a loved one. Infidelity brings back all of those childhood wounds for a person who was lied to or whose parents made promises they didn't keep. Those who were physically, sexually, or emotionally abused in previous relationships may be retraumatized when someone they have counted on betrays their trust and dependency. Judith Herman writes, 'Trauma forces the survivor to relive all her earlier struggles.... Traumatic life events, like other misfortunes, are especially merciless to those who are already troubled."

Wow. And yeah.

We might have thought those wounds were healed but if we're so destroyed by infidelity that we immediately go to the "we're not worthy" mindset, then we had just done a really good job of covering those wounds.

I thought I'd slain those particular dragons. Turns out, I'd kept the dragons at bay but they were still very much alive. And at the first sign of a crack in my armor, they were back, with their dragon eyes of judgement, and their dragon fire of shame and disgust.

The dragons, of course, are my own worst critics. The dragons, of course, are me.

My conversations with myself were more like indictments about everything I was doing wrong, from the careless remark I made at a cocktail party to the dust behind my refrigerator.

But I didn't recognize my own pain. I thought I'd healed.

I thought healed looked like a perfect marriage and well-behaved children and lots of friends and a busy social life. Add a successful writing career to show the world how accomplished I was. Turns out 'healed' looked an awful lot like perfection. And perfection, I've come to learn, looks an awful lot like a pretty band-aid over a festering wound of shame.

There are gifts in betrayal, if we're willing to look for them. For me, the re-trauma of infidelity revealed how shaky my sense of worth was – a worth based on achievement. Consequently, learning how to be kind to myself, which was nothing I'd ever allowed myself before, has transformed me.

I now know that healed is compassion and kindness and lack of judgement. Healed is about giving myself permission to be who I am, flaws and all. More than that, it's about giving everyone else permission too. It's knowing that I'll never be *fully* healed and that's okay because none of us are.

It's about forgiveness. Of those who've hurt me. But mostly, it's about forgiveness of myself.

Which is pretty much the same thing.

Revenge Affairs

Oooooh boy, it's tempting, isn't it? There was a guy who worked in my husband's office. We always had lots to say to each other. We made each other laugh. There was an unmistakable spark between us. And so, in the early days post D-Day when I was deep in the "what is wrong with me that he would cheat" stage of healing, I thought about how good it would be to feel wanted, to feel sexy, to feel anything other than agony. In short, I wanted to have an affair. With this guy.

Except that I also didn't want to. There would go my moral high ground, my "how could you do this?" righteousness. If I cheated too, then I wasn't any better, was I?

Besides, he was married. And I could never subject another woman to the pain I was in.

Finally, I knew that an affair would only compound my pain. That it might offer short-term relief. But that I would be left with a bigger mess on my hands than I already had.

This is exactly why one betrayed wife stayed home shortly after D-Day rather than attend a social event where she'd see an old crush. "I knew I was vulnerable."

Quite a few women have written on Betrayed Wives Club that they certainly thought about it. Most say they didn't. As one BWC member puts it, "I suppose I can understand why someone might want to do this but it's just flooding a house that's already been destroyed by a tornado."

Not all see it that way. A few copped to having a revenge affair though not a single one, in hindsight, thought it did anything other than make them feel worse.

BWC member Ashley puts it best: *Just don't do it. It may seem like a good idea but it really isn't. It won't help anything. Just have healthy fantasies...*

S

Sex After Infidelity

You might experience hysterical bonding (see also **Hysterical Bonding**) or you might enter a stage of celibacy, so repulsed by your husband that you can't imagine letting his naked body near you. I've yet to hear of a single betrayed wife whose sex life isn't altered in some way by news of her husband's infidelity. After a period of time, once the initial raw pain has given way to a dull ache, you might entertain the possibility that someday, you will have a "normal" (ha! again) sex life.

Cause here's the thing: sex after infidelity is like walking a field dotted with landmines. There are the mind movies (see also **Mind Movies**), there is sometimes his shame, there are the myriad insecurities that surface about our bodies, our sexuality, our desirability. All are like a bucket of water on a flickering libido. And all make sex after infidelity fraught.

None, however, have to do lasting damage.

Key to creating a healthy sex life after infidelity is slaying those demons. Therapy. Radical self-care. Honesty and transparency. Treating this like a second marriage with your first husband and getting to know one another again.

One betrayed wife decided to pledge (without telling her husband) to have sex with him once a day for a year. Her rationale was that, with time, it would again become routine in the best way. That the hurdles would fall away because she refused to see them. It worked. Two years later, she's still having daily sex. There's healing that remains to be done in the relationship, she admits, but their sex life is a source of pleasure for both.

After a period of hysterical bonding, I struggled to reconnect sexually with my husband. My husband's addiction to sex (see also **Sex Addiction**) was part of the problem. That remaining puzzle piece explained so much that had felt wrong in our relationship. It explained my sense of feeling objectified when we had sex (his sex addiction included a lot of porn). It explained his inappropriateness around sex, sometimes making frat-boy-type jokes that to him were funny but seemed childish and crude to me. It explained my awareness that he was often elsewhere emotionally when we had sex – present in body but not in spirit. Turns out, he needed fantasy to fuel his desire. A real-life wife – and mother of his children – didn't do the job, so to speak.

What's more, like so many of you after learning about a spouse's affair, my sexual identity was in tatters. I was so confused about our entire relationship – *what was real? what was fake?* – but especially our sexual relationship. I had believed myself desirable. I had thought of sex as connection. How could I have been so wrong?

In the meantime, my husband was in sexual addiction therapy and learning, for the first time, what healthy sexuality looked and felt like.

I was just trying to hold myself together. It was enough to get through the day. My bed and my pyjamas signalled to my husband that I was closed for business. I might as well have had a sign around my neck that read, "Leave me the hell alone."

I began to wonder about leaving. Not the "to hell with you, you bastard" kind of leaving (which I wholeheartedly support if that's what you want) but an "I want a healthy sexual relationship with someone who doesn't carry the same baggage" kind of leaving. I toyed with the idea of having a no-strings-attached sexual relationship outside of my marriage, feeling somewhat entitled given what my husband had put me through (see also **Revenge Affair**). But I knew I couldn't look myself in the mirror if I was violating my own value system.

Eventually, we found a therapist who specialized in sex. We saw him for about six months and inched forward incrementally.

All this time, however, we were rebuilding a marriage. Though I hold that sex is an important part of a marriage, I've come to recognize that it's not necessarily the glue that I'd always thought it was.

Marriages come in all shapes and forms and I felt no less married in a sex-less relationship than I had when we had frequent sex. In fact, I felt *more* married because we were so committed to making it work.

We realized that we were starting over with sex. Like shy teens, we had to come together in a way that we hadn't before, or at least not for a very long time. I've had to do a lot of work around my own body image, especially as my former marathoner's body has settled into middle age. I've learned that sex is many things – awkward, fun, amazing, uncomfortable – and that I don't need to feel threatened by any of that. The only person who expects me to constantly delight in bed is me. I've learned that, despite my conviction that I had no sexual hangups, I do.

I'm still learning. So is my husband.

Which is why I'm not sure that I have much to offer you beyond my own story about where I am right now: A middle-aged woman who's realizing that another chapter of her sex life is still being written. Perhaps you are too.

Sex Addiction

It took six months, following the initial discovery of my husband's affair, for him to confess the truth. It wasn't just one affair...it was dozens. He was, he confessed, a sex addict.

The night my husband told me, he curled up on the floor in the fetal position, sobbing. He insisted that I was disgusted with him and that he'd leave.

The truth is, along with the shock, came a relief. Relief because the missing piece was finally there to complete the puzzle I'd been agonizing over. *Why, why, why...?* I suddenly got it. While I wasn't exactly happy with this revelation, it gave me something I could understand. His affair had always baffled me. When I learned that their relationship wasn't really a relationship at all but a transaction...well, I could begin to let go of the questions that had plagued me.

But that was only the start.

My husband had already been working with a counsellor that specialized in sex addiction. Though he wasn't a CSAT (certified sex addiction therapist), he had set up a number of sex addiction treatment centers and was a recovered sex addict himself.

We spoke with him immediately and he gave me the Sex Addiction 101 chat. "Don't ask yourself what those women have that you don't," he advised me. "What they have, you don't want. They're very troubled people."

He explained to me that sex addiction is perhaps better termed an "intimacy disorder." The emphasis isn't on sex at all, really, but on the sex act as self-medicating. Most addicts use it to numb emotional pain, loneliness, anxiety. They turn to it the same way an alcoholic turns to a drink. But when the act is over, the addict can be overwhelmed with feelings of shame, guilt, self-loathing...which often leads to promises of abstinence, further acting out...and the cycle repeats.

I am, by no means, an expert. I am, however, someone with a front-row seat as this addiction is being wrestled with in the public arena.

Up close, sex addiction isn't so different from any other addiction. An unhealthy and often dangerous way of numbing oneself. I view the public's perception of sex addiction similarly to how alcoholism was viewed in the early part of the 20th century, until it became better understood. In fact, the World Health Organization just classified sex addiction as a mental health issue, specifically a "compulsive sexual health disorder" based on a list of criteria that include: repetitive sexual activities becoming the focus of the person's life, numerous unsuccessful efforts to reduce sexual behaviour and continued sexual activity despite deriving little satisfaction from it.

My husband, along with treatment from his therapist, attended a 12-step program – Sex Addicts Anonymous – for a year. He developed a treatment plan that included how to manage temptation, how to deal with relapse (he was required to tell me), abstinence from porn and masturbation (abstinence even from sex for 30 days). He was something of a star student. He was so disgusted with his own behaviour and so motivated for change that recovery, though not easy, was straightforward. He didn't relapse, though plenty do. He was tempted, at times, to view porn, but didn't cave.

I attended a program for partners of sex addicts, though it fizzled out after a few meetings. I found support through reading everything I could get my hands on. And I know that growing up with an alcoholic mother who found sobriety in church basements via AA helped me understand my husband's addiction and, to some extent, avoid taking responsibility for it. I had already walked that walk with my mother's addiction.

Our couples counsellor encouraged us to participate in a disclosure session. It's a common response to discovery of a partner's sex addiction and requires the addict disclosing everything he engaged in while acting out. Every. Single. Thing.

I insisted my husband agree to this, which, though reticent, he did. But because I had already asked him so many questions – and he had answered – I decided that I didn't want to know any more. It was enough that my husband agreed to participate because I knew how excruciating it would be for him.

Sex addiction is devastating and consequences can sometimes be more complicated. STDs are more likely, arrest is possible, finances can be decimated by use of prostitutes and massage parlours.

But treatment is available – and crucial – for both the addict and his partner.

Silence Around Infidelity

"When we discover that someone we trusted can be trusted no longer, it forces us to reexamine the universe, to question the whole instinct and concept of trust. For a while, we are thrust back onto some bleak, jutting ledge, in a dark pierced by sheets of fire, swept by sheets of rain, in a world before kinship, or naming, or tenderness exist; we are brought close to formlessness." - Adrienne Rich, *On Lies, Secrets and Silence*

Cheating is everywhere – in songs, in movies, in books, in

our workplaces, our neighborhoods. And yet we rarely see the consequences of cheating. We might hear of the divorce and the reason behind it. Or we might know, through whispers, that someone is dealing with a spouse's affair, though we're more likely to see the brave face than the tear-streaked one.

Hiding the true impact of infidelity, however, makes it seem so much more benign than it is, so much more matter-of-fact. Less mind-blowing than mundane. Ho-hum, another cheating spouse. Tell me something new.

And then it happens to us and our world blows apart. Which leaves us with this bizarre disconnect between what the world seems to think of infidelity ("kick him out and move on") and the devastation it inflicts on us, our families, our friends, our work.

As Adrienne Rich puts it: "It forces us to reexamine the universe."

Infidelity is about being forced to examine our place in the universe. Our perceptions of the world. Is the world a safe place? Who can we believe? Who am I? And, just who the hell is he? Who is this stranger I'm married to who behaved in a way I could have never imagined?

There is no way around this. We can leave the marriage, which is a perfectly viable option. We can choose to stay and rebuild a second marriage with our first husband, another perfectly viable option. We can sweep it under the proverbial rug and step around it or over it or under it, though that's not such a viable option.

But, to truly heal from it, we must go through it. We must perch on Rich's "bleak, jutting ledge" and acknowledge how deep the injury goes. But then we must slowly pull ourselves back, examining all the while what this means to us, how it impacts who we are, and honoring what we need to move forward in our lives. We must learn that we can – and should

– trust ourselves. Infidelity thrusts us onto that ledge. But we don't have to stay there.

It is my hope that, someday, infidelity is recognized as the cancer it is, and treated much the same way. With treatment and concern, casseroles and compassion. That it's publicly acknowledged and examined so that those of us affected by it don't have to perch on that ledge alone. That there's support and strength from those who recognize the true impact of infidelity and aren't afraid to reach out a hand.

Spyware

I can barely post to Instagram without the help of one of my teens, so I'm hardly a candidate for installing spyware (though companies promise it takes less than 10 minutes). I had considered monitoring my husband's cyber-life. Thing is, it's unethical, if not illegal (generally, you must notify the person on whom you're spying, which kinda defeats the purpose, no?).

It's tempting, I know. And plenty of cads have been caught through snooping. But it still feels...wrong.

There are exceptions. Porn/sex addicts might want keyloggers or other surveillance installed to keep them straight in the early days of recovery.

But for everyone else? Steer clear of the moral/legal minefield, establish clear boundaries of your own, and gather skills to be able to have these tough conversations.

Stalking the OW on Social Media

Thanks to social media, it's easier than ever to keep tabs on the OW. But easy is not the same as healthy. One of the most common sources of misery cited by the women who come to Betrayed Wives Club is their obsession with stalking the OW on social media.

Social media, of course, is not real life. It is, as one friend puts it, the "highlight reel, not the outtakes." We're not seeing the Other Woman, we're seeing a polished version of her, including sappy quotes about generosity and kindness, photos of her beaming smile, one that puts forth the fantasy that her life is perfect and beautiful and that she has shaken off any pain associated with her affair .

C'mon, secret sisters. We know this is bullshit. Still, we stalk. And we simmer. And we feel so cheated. Because even though our own social media doesn't include selfies of us crumpled on the floor sobbing, even though we aren't posting quotes about vengeance and bitterness, even though we post our highlight reel, not our outtakes, we still get sucked in to this idea that her life really is fine. That she really has moved on without a thought for the damage she helped inflict. That she really is that happy.

I doubt it.

It's also beside the point. The point is that stalking keeps you focussed on her and her life rather than you and your life. It keeps you hooked into her rather than recognizing that she's extraneous. What she brought to the affair are two things: availability and willingness, and neither of those traits is hard to find. She's not special. OWs are a dime a dozen.

Shift the focus back to you and your real (not curated) life. Stop tormenting yourself with glossy images of her. She does not belong in your life. Click delete.

STDs (Sexually Transmitted Diseases), Getting Tested for

One of the most humiliating days of my life was sitting in the waiting room at my local clinic, along with the hungover college students, to get tested. I was shaking with anger. The nurse was compassionate and gentle. And she nodded knowingly when I told her why I was there and who, exactly, was to blame.

Even if your husband insists he was "safe," even if says "nothing happened," even if you feel physically healthy and there's no sign of issues, get tested. Most of the stories I've heard turned out fine. But not all. And if you have something, you want it treated now. Tell the doctor or nurse why you're there. Ask for help if you need it. If you think you might need pharmaceutical help to get through, tell him/her that. If you're even toying with the idea that the world would be better off without you, tell him/her that. Ask about support groups, ask about therapists who take insurance or who have sliding rates. Enlist this person's help.

Stay or Go

"Should I stay or should I go" is the question that seems to be at the heart of just about every betrayed wife in the days/weeks/months following D-Day.

It's an impossible question to answer for anyone else. We each need to walk our own path to healing. But there is a pervasive cultural message that has even further damaged betrayed wives and it is this: Women who stay are doormats.

The women who struggle the most with their choice to stay are those who beat themselves up for not leaving because staying feels like weakness. Thing is, I don't know a single woman who stayed who isn't a fierce and total badass. These aren't women who roll over or turn a blind eye. They're women who demand that their wayward partner step up and take responsibility for the pain he's caused and fight like hell to rebuild their marriage. Does that sound like weakness to you? Cause it sure as hell sounds like strength to me. So it's important to cut through the noise in your head when you're trying to figure out what you want to do. Make sure it's YOUR choice and not something you feel you "should" do, whether that "should" is to stay because it would break your mother's heart to have a divorced daughter, or whether that "should" is to leave because of some culturally prescribed bullshit that tells us the only response to infidelity is to kick him to the curb and wash your hands of him.

Nonetheless, staying isn't for the faint of heart. The other massive barrier to staying in a marriage is the sheer terror that he's going to do this again. And it's a legitimate fear. As the saying goes, the best predictor of future behavior is past behavior. He's cheated on you before, what's to stop him from doing it again? One of the consistent questions I get on Betrayed Wives Club is "How can I be sure he won't cheat on me again?" And my answer is, you can't.

It doesn't offer much comfort, does it? I wish I could give you some sort of guarantee. That if you do A or B, then he will never, ever cheat again. Beware of anyone who tells you that you can affair-proof your marriage. You can make cheating less likely but you can never have a guarantee, no matter what anyone tells you, including your spouse. Lots of people who cheat, including women, are as shocked as anyone by their behavior. People don't necessarily make the decision to cheat all at once. They make the decision to go out for lunch with that work colleague who makes them laugh. Or they agree to after-work drinks and start sharing details of your marriage. Or they flirt with the Starbucks barista. It's tiny lines that are easily dismissed as harmless until the line that isn't. But by then, so many lines have been crossed that the final one seems almost inevitable. And THAT is where change needs to occur.

It isn't about a spouse who promises not to cheat again. It's about a spouse who understands the danger in flirting, in not mentioning his wife, in holding someone's gaze a little too long. It's about a spouse who realizes the many lines he crossed while telling himself that he wasn't doing anything wrong. It's about a spouse who finally gets that if you wouldn't do what you're doing with your wife watching you, you shouldn't be doing it at all.

Sometimes, however, we need to give ourselves permission to do nothing, to absorb the shock, tend to our wounds and wait until we're more clear-headed so that we're responding rather than reacting. We can also make some observations.

For instance, when your focus is on the time and energy you've invested in an endeavour (or person) rather than the love, joy, and gratification you've experienced, you might be settling. It doesn't matter if you've spent five years or 30 with someone, if many of those years have been unfulfilling.

When you're rationalizing why you should stay put rather than going for what you truly want, you might be settling. Sometimes we need to stay put in order to create circumstances that allow us to leave safely (see **Escape Plan**). But be honest with yourself about whether those reasons for staying are legitimate or excuses that allow indecision. If you stay, make sure that's a choice and not an abdication of choice. Similarly, if you leave, make sure it's a choice and not something you feel you should do because our culture insists that "once a cheater, always a cheater," or that anyone who stays with an unfaithful spouse is pathetic.

Perhaps the wisest question we can ask is that age-old Dear Ann Landers nugget: *Am I better off with him or without him?*

As Esther Perel puts it, are you ready to have a second marriage with the same man? Because the first marriage is over and dead.

I finally felt comfortable rebuilding my marriage when I

realized my husband was committed to dealing with his issues, even if I left. He told me that he wanted to be able to look himself in the mirror and feel proud of who he was. That's husband material.

Stories, The Power of Telling Our

We all have our D-Day stories, don't we? We go back and pore over the days, weeks, years that led up to D-Day. *Was he cheating when I was visiting my sister? Was he cheating when I was pregnant? Was he cheating when we were with the kids in Florida?*

We beg for details to help us fill out our stories. What we don't know, we invent. The Other Woman was a gymnast in bed. She had long legs. She laughed charmingly at his stupid jokes. She had long blonde hair.

And the mind movies are devastating. We lie in bed playing them over and over again. Or they ambush us when we hear a certain song, drive past a certain restaurant, notice a certain time of year.

Thing is, we weren't there. We will never ever know what it was really like. Nothing is ever really as fabulous as we think it is. Not the celebrity lives we envy in magazines. Not the other moms' lives with their kids who never seem to whine. Not the Other Woman with her imagined sexual sorcery.

Which is why we need to tell our stories with ourselves cast as the heroine. Maybe a tragic heroine, but a heroine nonetheless. Our stories can save us, if we let them. I'm not talking about creating a fiction, necessarily. But there's a ton of brain science about the value of stories in healing trauma. It's why rape survivors need to tell their stories. It's why plane crash victims need to tell their stories. Over and over and over.

And it's why we betrayed wives need to tell our stories.

It's how we make sense of what's happened to us. And it's how we re-insert ourselves back into a narrative that we've been written out of. Our husband might have conveniently ignored our role in his life; the OW might be able to pretend we don't exist. But we don't have to buy that story. No way. We can tell our own.

Our story begins and ends with us – fighting like hell for our bodies, our hearts and souls. Ours is a story about a resurrection, a rebirth. It's about a woman who refuses to give up on herself, who refuses to accept others' stories. We are whole. Not bit players in another's story but stars in our own.

Tell your story. The whole truth of it. Tell it as many times as you can to anyone who will hold it in their own hearts, without judgement, without flinching at your pain. Tell it until it fits your life and resolves the past. It is yours and it will be your rebirth.

Stupid Shit Cheaters Say

A popular thread on Betrayed Wives Club is where wives share the absolute stupidest things their husbands have said to them in defending their indefensible actions. A sampling:

"I felt bad and guilty Every Time."

"If it makes you feel better, I couldn't get it up the first time. I was so nervous."

"I knew that talking to another woman online and meeting her in real life was wrong, but I didn't realize it was cheating."

"It's a pity you're not taking it as an adventure. We're both young. You look good. You'll easily meet somebody else."

"I thought you didn't love me anymore."

"I thought you had an affair a few years earlier."

"It wasn't fun, it was a burden."

"I never meant to hurt you. I thought I was protecting you by making sure you would never find out."

"I never talked bad about you or let any of them talk bad about you. They all knew I loved my wife."

"I didn't have sex with other women because I was attracted to any of them or the sex was good. I had sex with them because it was convenient."

"We should all just be friends."

"You know, over 60% of marriages experience infidelity."

My advice to these cheaters. Stop. Talking.

Suffering, How to Release

In the hours and weeks and months following D-Day, we exist in an excruciating state of suspension. It hurts to breathe. It hurts to wake up. It hurts when he walks out the door and it hurts when he stays.

Everything hurts.

But, sometimes what we do to ourselves after betrayal hurts us even more.

We spend our days longing for things to be different. *If only he hadn't taken the job where he met her. If only we had insisted he stay home that night. If only we had seen what was happening sooner.* Suffering, say the wise, is our attachment to the idea that now could be otherwise. Spending our days wishing things were different keeps us tethered to our suffering. Suffering doesn't vanish once we say to ourselves, *Well, this is my reality so I might as well deal with it.* But it moves us toward less suffering. We get back our power when we accept our situation. When we let go of our idea that things should be different, we free ourselves of the Gordian knot that keeps us stuck.

How?

Practice. If your self-esteem is a bit shaky (and whose isn't after being cheated on?), then you build it up. You remind yourself that *his* cheating isn't about *your* value. Rather it devalues him, not you.

You switch up your affair fantasies. It's more likely true that the affair you're imagining was a bit of a nightmare. I mostly hear stories of kinda crappy sex, miserable and/or unhinged Other Women, shame and self-disgust, feeling trapped. It's just as easy to change the channel in your brain to this less idealized (and more accurate) depiction. Imagine an Other Woman with room-clearing flatulence. An embarrassing laugh. Whatever else makes her human and less threatening.

Try to catch yourself when you begin wandering down the "if only...." road. Our life is not sliding doors. We're shaped by our choices and those of others. If, in hindsight, we want to review some of our choices with the clear eyes that come with time and perspective, then do it. We can all learn to pay more attention to our gut or our intuition. We can recognize when we're doing things we don't want to do.

But, mostly, we can release the idea that we had any real control over a decision that our partner made. We didn't choose to cheat, he did. And he did it for reasons of his own that he, if he wants us to consider giving him a second chance, needs to discern for himself.

Leave that with him.

Focus on you.

Wonderful, devastated you.

Suicide, Thinking of

Heartbreak. Anguish. Desperation. Such need for a lifeline.

I wish I had the expertise and resources to reach those

who see no way out of this pain. I wish I could restore your will to live when you're drowning in sorrow.

I pray that the words written here act as a tether, keeping you rooted in this world until the pain inevitably subsides and you realize the strength you've always had to carry on, to wait until tomorrow (or the next tomorrow) reveals its beauty.

I considered ending my life. I didn't think I could live with the pain for a second longer. I couldn't imagine a future that didn't include this level of agony.

But I had children. And I had been a child when my own mother attempted suicide. I know now that she attempted suicide for the same reason that I considered it. The pain felt greater than her ability to carry it. Her imagined tomorrow held only more pain.

But to the child me, my mother's attempted suicide wasn't about her rejecting her pain but about her rejecting *me*. I concluded that *I* wasn't worth living for. It has taken me many, many years to value myself. To value my own life.

No matter how deep my pain following D-Day, I wouldn't risk putting that on my children.

At that moment, I might not have valued my own life but I valued theirs.

And then an interesting thing happened.

I asked myself what it was about them that made them valuable. Was it their beauty? Their intelligence? Their ability to make me smile? Their creativity? What did they *do* that made their lives worthy?

Of course, it wasn't anything they did. It was their being. My children's lives had value simply because they existed.

And I realized that my own life had value simply because I existed.

Yes, I was in a horribly dark place. Darker than I'd ever been. But some of that darkness came from my own secret self. Some of that darkness came not just from what my husband had done but from *the story I was telling myself about what he had done.* The story that included me not being pretty enough, not being sexy enough, not being worth loving.

And by admitting those secrets to myself I was able to examine them and see that they were untrue. Just as my children are worth loving because they just *are*...so am I worth loving because I *am*. And so, my beloved reader, are *you*.

I can imagine all the protestations. *But you don't know me*, you might be thinking. *You don't know how bitchy I can be. You don't know how fat I've become. You don't know how many mistakes I've made in life.*

How often I've failed.

No, I don't. But I know how often *I* have...and that's pretty much the same thing.

So while I don't have a hotline or a lifeline or any other way to reach you when you are in that dark, scary place where your secret self is longing for an escape from the pain, I do have this: I'm not in that place anymore where it hurts to breathe. My kids showed me that all life is sacred. That we are enough.

I hope you can remember that. I hope you can begin to let that secret self out to express her pain, to tell the story of her long journey to this place, and to know that the story isn't over. That it will include healing.

Your secret self will make some people uncomfortable and they will wish you would shut up about it. But your secret self is a prophet, leading you out of the darkness...and lighting the way for countless others.

T

Tears

All I know is that after 10 years of being sober, with huge support to express my pain and anger and shadow, the grief and tears didn't wash me away. They gave me my life back! They cleansed me, baptized me, hydrated the earth at my feet. They brought me home, to me, to the truth of me.

Those words are from the wonderful writer Anne Lamott.

How often do we cry those tears and then feel ourselves cleansed? Our problem might still exist, the pain might still be there, but it feels smaller. Somehow we feel as though we've paid respect to our pain. Acknowledged its legitimacy.

Women's tears have had a bad rap. Men, having typically been told since they were toddlers that "boys don't cry" have long buried their sadness, expressing it instead in anger or addiction or affairs. We women were given a bit more time to get our emotions under control. It was acceptable to cry until our teens. And then, because it made people uncomfortable – boyfriends, bosses, mothers – we blinked the tears back. Otherwise we risked being called manipulative, "turning on the waterworks," too sensitive, *emotional*.

My mother often looked at me, her hypersensitive child, like I was some sort of alien. "Why are you crying?" she would ask me, curious. Why was I crying? Well...my mother didn't understand me, she drank too much, I felt lonely and, well, sad. But I got the message. Tears were weakness. If I couldn't stop them, they were to be hidden.

But those tears saved me. I *felt* my feelings instead of numbing them. My mom eventually unearthed her own pain but not before she'd stormed through a decade, cauterizing her sadness with alcohol.

Thanks, but I'll take a cup of tears. A thousand cups.

D-Day and the subsequent months of anguish brought forth an ocean of tears.

My therapist, soaked to the knees in my tears, told me that we have a finite number of tears to cry before we're cleansed. You, she told me, haven't yet reached that number. Let the tears flow and trust that the day will come when they will dry up.

That permission was crucial. Equally crucial was the understanding that, eventually, the tears would dry. Implicit in that is the recognition that the sadness will lift. But for now...cry.

The grief, Lamott promises, won't wash you away. It will baptize you into this world that holds pain but also love and joy. Those tears will, if you let them, bring you to the truth of you. That you are whole. That you are worthy. That you are sane and human and okay and sad. Right now, you are sad.

Telling the Other Woman's Husband (or Partner)

A few years ago, an advice columnist for *O, the Oprah Magazine* responded to a writer who wondered if she should tell a woman she knew that her husband was cheating. She wrote:

"Don't say a word to anyone. To begin with, it could be that your friend's daughter already knows and is trying to handle things privately—or at least without any involvement from her mother. It could also be that his cheating heart will come to its senses before his wife finds out, in which case you could end up hurting a lot of people for what may have been no more than one terrible transgression. Finally, nobody ever knows what's really going on inside someone else's marriage; perhaps these two have some sort of "don't ask, don't tell" arrangement. Are any of these scenarios likely? I don't know, and neither do you. The point is that they're all plausible—so keep quiet."

This advice is common. It's also wrong.

I responded to the columnist with this:

When I was young and out shopping with my mother, I spotted my best friend's dad. "Hey, there's Mr. Sutton (not his real name)," I said. And then, faltering, "But that's not Mrs. Sutton." My mom quickly shushed me, making it clear that I saw nothing and was to say nothing.

Back at the Sutton home was Mrs. Sutton, who had no "don't ask, don't tell" policy. There was no "open marriage." Mr. Sutton didn't "come to his senses" before his wife found out.

Instead, there was only a bewildered Mrs. Sutton, wondering why her husband never seemed to be home and why he found fault with everything she did. She had no reason to suspect she should be insisting on protection when she had sex with her husband. She had no reason to speak with a lawyer to ensure her self-employed husband wasn't hiding assets.

So when he asked for a divorce so he could marry not-Mrs.-Sutton, she was blindsided.

Fast forward 33 years and I'm in Mrs. Sutton's shoes with a cheating husband in a culture that often recommends looking the other way. So are millions of women who've visited my website.

Before I'd been cheated on, I would have given exactly the advice you gave. Don't get involved. There might be agreements in place, etc. Which is true. There might be, though I doubt it. And while we're looking the other way, the betrayed wife might contract an STD as more than a few women I know have. One woman, who contracted cervical cancer, will never know if it's because of the STD her husband passed along thanks to one of his "terrible transgressions."

A betrayed wife might choose to get pregnant again, go back to school, agree to quit her job and become a stay-at-home mom. In other words, they might continue to make decisions based on believing they have a solid marriage and a dependable partner, when they have neither.

At the very least, betrayed wives feel utterly humiliated when they learn that others knew of their husband's affair and said nothing. It compounds the shame we already feel for not knowing it ourselves, for not suspecting. If we do suspect and have no real evidence to back up our suspicions, we're routinely told we're crazy. "Of course not," our husbands scoff. "She's just a friend/work colleague/old college acquaintance." And so we silence that voice. I don't know a single betrayed wife who doesn't wish some benevolent person – friend, stranger, doesn't matter – hadn't taken them aside or written a letter and gently told them what he/she knew. Something like, "I hope I'm off-base here but I saw your husband having lunch with a woman and it looked a little cozy. I just wanted you to know." Or "I will keep my mouth shut to everybody else, but I recently discovered that your husband is having an affair. I'm here for you in whatever way you need."

Sure the wife might respond with anger. She might insist

that you're wrong. Her own head will be spinning. She'll be in shock. If there is some sort of agreement (though I highly doubt it), she can respond with "I know about that. But thanks for telling me."

Telling the cheater himself gives him the chance to go underground, to cover up his tracks, to lay low until the crisis blows over. He might prepare the wife to dismiss anyone else's disclosure with "Oh, I ran into Marilyn when I was out with Joe's girlfriend buying him a gift. She looked at me kinda funny. She's such a gossip."

Being cheated on is one of the loneliest experiences. Everybody pretends it isn't happening while your world is caving in. It's not uncommon for people who've been cheated on to experience post-trauma symptoms: hypervigilance, flashbacks, nightmares.

Nobody should take any pleasure in telling someone her spouse is cheating. You're right that it's a no-win situation. But that doesn't mean it's not the right thing to do. It's just not the easy thing.

Time, How Much Will It Take to Heal

Time is a four-letter word as the minutes feel like days and the days like lifetimes. Three to five years is the general estimate for getting past betrayal, say the experts. Three to five YEARS, most of us scream when we first hear it. YEARS?? We were hoping a few months of tears and recriminations and somehow this would be behind us.

But though I stand by my insistence that time is a great healer, healing isn't a passive exercise in watching the minute hands sweep. It's not enough to simply mark the days off a calendar, like a prisoner awaiting release. Those of us seeking relief from suffering need to fight like hell for it.

It sounds exhausting, doesn't it? Surviving feels Herculean and now I'm asking you to fight like hell. Seriously? Well, yes.

Not right away. Not without taking a break now and again, like a caterpillar inside a chrysalis.

But only we can reach for our own salvation. Nobody is going to ride in on a white horse and save us. (And frankly, be wary of anyone promising to do that.)

Cry. Rant and rave. Write your story out until you're spent. And always, always reach.

What are we reaching for? What do we hold onto when we don't know whether to stay or go? When we don't know whether to believe the pretty words on our partner's lips that sound so much like the pretty lies we believed?

We reach for healing. Healing that looks like wholeness, with or without him. Healing that comes from a heart strengthened where it was broken and capable of deep self-love and compassion.

We find that healing within our own determination to survive this. To know that, no matter how shattered we feel today, there's still tomorrow. And the next tomorrow. And that one of these tomorrows, we'll feel a crack open in the darkness and tiniest sliver of light will show through. But we have to be looking for it. We have to be reaching for it. Through radical self-care (that will be called selfishness by those around us unaccustomed to seeing us love ourselves. Ignore them). Through compassion and forgiveness for ourselves for whatever we deem our failings to be – we should have known, we should have handled it better, we should have done things differently. Maybe. I've yet to meet a soul who's lived his/her life perfectly. Let it go.

We heal through sharing our stories. We heal through the support of others who remind us that we're lovely and lovable and loved.

We heal by reaching as far as we can. Some days that

reach will be short. But that's okay. Because we'll have other days when our reach will extend into a future that includes the recognition that we are not where we were. That we feel whole. That we – yes, let's say it! – we have healed.

Gabby, one of our club members, puts it this way:

As much as you don't want to hear this, you just want this pain to disappear, it won't. It won't be an overnight cure. You must understand that.

The pain is real and it's there for a reason. You care. You are hurting. The pain will lessen as the days, weeks, months, years pass. It may not seem like it, but it does. I'm living proof. I am almost two years post D-Day, and am into my second separation, which looks permanent, and I have survived, and I am living, and the pain has lessened.

Time Out, How to Take A

For weeks, I would shake my husband awake in the middle of night to badger him. I would insist that he couldn't leave for work if I needed to "talk" to him. In short, I was holding him emotionally hostage. And nothing I was doing was actually making me feel better.

My husband's therapist told him that he was allowed to call 'time outs' if I wouldn't back down when asked. At first, I balked. How dare he get to decide when I had to stop? He was the reason I was in this emotional maelstrom! But my husband pointed out that our "talks" weren't helpful and often escalated to screaming and name calling. He knew that I wanted to protect our kids, as much as possible, from what was happening. And though I felt insulted and further abandoned, there was a teensy bit of sanity in my brain that knew he was right.

Time outs are often the terrain of parents trying to help children manage their behaviour. But infidelity often takes us back to those huge emotions that feel impossible to manage, that cripple us, that render us blind with fury and pain.

When our feelings are bigger than our ability to manage them (as I often say to my children), that's our clue that we or our partner need a time out:

Here's how:

1. Notice your feelings and behaviours: Are you overwhelmed by emotion? Is your mind racing? Is your voice getting louder? Are you having physical symptoms of overwhelm — tingling, panic. Are you throwing things? Slamming doors? Refusing to let your partner leave a room or your home?

2. Tell your husband that you need a time out. It's important that you both agree to time outs beforehand so that he knows that a time out doesn't mean the matter is settled. It simply means you're taking a step away until you can come back calmly.

3. Set the limits in advance. How long will the time out last? Where will you be while you calm down?

4. After the agreed upon time has elapsed, check in with yourself. If you need more time, then let your partner know. If not, then return when you said you would.

5. Resume the conversation or schedule a mutually agreed upon time to resume.

Tough Conversation, How to Have A

Our trip had not started off well. My husband was overworked and grumpy. I was overtired and resentful. I had a laundry list of things that had been building up that I wanted to talk to him about but hadn't found the time.

Neither of us had been doing any self-care and our attitudes showed it.

We snarked at each other in the airport. He snapped at the kids. I chastised him for snapping at the kids.

We might have been heading to a tropical paradise but none of us seemed very happy about it.

Two days in, we finally found ourselves alone on the beach. It would have been easy to tell myself that now wasn't the time. That I should just enjoy the breeze and the sunshine.

I swallowed hard. "I need you to listen to me," I said.

So often, we find ourselves in a situation that takes us right back to a terrible moment. A song. A certain model of car. We pass a restaurant or a motel or a massage parlour. And it feels like a kick in the gut. Our throats constrict. Our hearts, literally, ache.

There's not much we can do about triggers but wait them out. But what we can do is have those tough conversations with our partners about them.

It's tempting to not bring them up. Our partners, especially if they're still new to this tough conversation stuff, will almost inevitably disappoint us with their response. They'll get defensive. They'll try to shut us down. They'll ask us if we're ever going to get over this. They'll get silent. They might get angry.

All of those are countermoves (see also **Countermoves**) and are the response of someone who can't handle his own feelings. Someone who just wants this to go away.

We know that doesn't work.

Have the tough conversation anyway.

Even if you're the only one talking, have the tough conversation.

"I need you to listen to me."

"I want you to know something."

"It matters to me that you know this because I need support."

"I'm hurting and I need to share this with you."

However you phrase it, give words to your pain.

Not to make him feel bad (though that might be an inevitable part of this) but because he's your partner and you're going through this together.

Not to cast blame but to seek support and compassion.

It takes practice. If he responds in a way that's disappointing or hurtful, talk about it. Tell him you don't want to hear excuses. That you don't want to be talked out of your feelings. Tell him he doesn't even need to say a thing. Tell him that this was tough for you and that you need a friend right now. That's it. A friend. Not a therapist and certainly not an adversary. An ally.

It's fraught, of course. The person you most want to help you through is the person responsible for the pain you're in.

Fighting back tears, I proceeded to tell my husband how his attitude sometimes hurts me and the kids. I stuck to "me" statements. "I feel hurt when..." "The kids feel frustrated when..."

I pointed out that he seemed so annoyed with me. That I feel small and stupid.

He listened. He hadn't realized how his stress came out as annoyance with me. That wasn't how he felt.

He shared some of his own frustrations with work, with our kids, with me. I listened to him.

By the time he got up to get us a couple of margaritas a half-hour later, I felt lighter.

Pain is heavy.

It doesn't always work out quickly or easily. Sometimes we need to take a break and walk away and come back to the conversation a day or two later. Sometimes it takes each of us some time to really digest what the other is saying. Old habits die hard and we get defensive. Simple truth is we don't want to hear about the other's pain, especially when it triggers our own shame in creating it.

But...marriage is tough. Marriage after betrayal is especially tough. And having these tough conversations can create a foundation beneath you that will hold you both up as you move forward. Being able to listen and say little more than "I'm so sorry you had to go through that" or "If I could go back in time and un-do this, I would" or "Thank you for sharing that. What do you need from me?" goes a long way toward shoring up that foundation.

But you cannot rebuild a healthy marriage without, eventually, learning how to have these tough conversations. Without learning to really hear each other's pain.

Trickle Truth

It goes like this: A woman who has discovered a partner's affair Googles "my husband cheated" or "hurting wife" and is led to my site where she posts about her husband admitting that he kissed a co-worker and can she ever forgive him and how can she believe that's as far as it went. And my stomach sinks. Because the chances that he just kissed a co-worker are about the same as the chances that I'm going to lose 10 pounds on a cookie and margarita diet.

It's called the "trickle truth" and most of us are familiar with the experience, if not the term. In my case, I asked my husband if he was having an affair with his assistant at work. Only once, many years ago, he said. And then, after a few days of my relentless questioning, he admitted that it had been more than once and that it had lasted a few months. With further interrogation, he confessed to an affair that had begun and ended a few times. Finally, six months later when he'd secretly been in treatment for sex addiction, I got the whole truth, mostly because his therapist insisted he tell me.

Trickle truth causes massive damage. It might sound harmless but it further erodes trust and exacerbates post-trauma by prolonging the agony of discovering a partner's betrayal. So often, betrayed women say it's not the sex that they feel so betrayed by, it's the lies. It is a deliberate deception, a hiding of certain information, a refusal to come clean.

Trickle truth is the slow release of information, each bit more incriminating than what's come before, and usually only disclosed under duress. It is borne of self-preservation. A guy, newly revealed as a cheater and, perhaps, realizing what he actually stands to lose, is trying to come off as less of an asshole. So they "just kissed" a coworker. Or it was "just once." "Just" should be struck from the cheater's vocabulary. There is nothing "just" about this.

Or cheaters convince themselves that they're protecting us. The whole truth would hurt us too much and so they dole it out, minimizing what really happened out of some misguided belief that they can mask the extent of the betrayal and keep us from a total shattering of our heart.

It doesn't work. Somehow, the truth will emerge. It might be within hours or days, or even years. And then, with that revelation, any trust that might have been painstakingly rebuilt will be gone.

There's no real fix for a guy engaged in trickle truth other than to appeal to any sense of decency he might have left. We deserve full honesty and a complete accounting of his behaviour. He owes us that. If he was interested in "protecting" us, he wouldn't have cheated. If he was hoping that his behaviour wouldn't have consequences, well, that was foolish.

Trickle truth is lies. And as so many betrayed wives will say, it's isn't the sex that's the worst of it, it's the lies.

Triggers

They're everywhere. A song comes on the radio and suddenly our heart is pounding because it's the song that was playing when we got the news. A certain model car speeds past and we freeze because it's the same car *she* drove. Or we spot someone ahead and are absolutely sure it's her and we feel light-headed and have tunnel vision and ohmygod are we going to have a panic attack right here in the cereal aisle of the grocery store?

Triggers are incredibly common after any sort of trauma, including betrayal. And they're tough to manage because they ambush us. We can't anticipate when or where they'll show up.

One day, a few years after D-Day, my husband came home from work and, as usual, gave me a recap of his day. He mentioned that he'd had lunch with a salesperson, noting that he'd offered up, what he thought, was a smart way this person's company could improve their business.

In the telling of this story, something was, to me, notable. He mentioned he'd had lunch with A salesperson. Singular. But as the story went on, he didn't refer to this salesperson as a him or a her but as they.

My body tensed. My heart beat faster. My mind raced.

I knew, without asking, that this was because this salesperson with whom he'd had lunch was a she. And I feared that there was something about this she that made my husband avoid any discussion of it.

So I asked him whether this they was a male or female. He told me what I already knew.

And then I screeched something about how I couldn't believe he'd lied to me and was this ever going to end and how I can't trust him.

He panicked and doubled down in attempts to placate me. He hadn't lied, he said. (Bullshit, I said!). He just didn't want me to draw the wrong conclusion, that there was nothing. (Heard that before, I said.)

In short, we both blew it.

Our counsellor offered us a far better approach.

She said my response was normal and made it clear to my husband that when he seems to be hiding ANYTHING, that's a huge trigger for me. It takes me right back to where I was when I found out. That it's the deceit that's the trigger, not necessarily the lunch with a female.

And then she told me to ask my husband what I really wanted to know.

It's so hard for me to open myself up to vulnerability. It has been a lifelong struggle and though I'm better, it's really, really hard.

Nonetheless, heart pounding, I asked: "Are you attracted to this woman?" No. "Is there anything going on that you would not want me to know about?" No.

He insisted, got defensive, said all sorts of unhelpful things about how she's older and more mother-like to him and how he's never sure if he's allowed to be attracted to anyone but me ever again even if he never intends to act on it and on and on until our counsellor stopped him. She told him, pointedly, that this wasn't helpful.

And then she guided him through what was helpful. Reminding me that he's working hard on his issues so that he never again betrays me. Reminding me that he doesn't want to be that guy ever again. Reminding me that he loves me and values our marriage and family. That he won't jeopardize that.

I cried. But then I practically floated out of that session. It empowered both of us. Me, to realize that allowing myself to ask for what I needed and opening myself to vulnerability isn't going to always mean hurt. Him, to realize that by reminding me that he's NOT that guy anymore is also reminding himself that he's come a long way. That it's a source of pride about who he is now instead of a source of shame about what he did.

Triggers can appear no matter how far we are along the

path of healing. And when they appear, they transport us right back to that horrible moment when our world spiralled out of control and we felt alone and scared. Trusting ourselves to ask for what we need in that moment, and our spouse to offer it to us, binds us closer together. Triggers can be teachers.

Trauma

Penelope Trunk, a blogger who was in the World Trade Center when the towers fell on September 11, 2001, knows a thing or two about trauma.

We women, who've been betrayed by exactly the people we trusted with our hearts and bodies, also know a thing or two about trauma.

Here's what Trunk has to (brilliantly) say about trauma:

The way to deal with post-traumatic stress is to tell your story over and over again. The theory is that when you are in the moment of trauma, you have to turn off all your emotions to get yourself through it. After the fact, in order to stop having nightmares and panic attacks, you have to experience the emotions you missed.

And this is the step that so many cheaters, including reformed cheaters, just can't get.

We need to talk about what happened to us. We are *desperate* to talk about it.

It doesn't prolong our pain. It does exactly the opposite. It doesn't deepen our pain. It does just the opposite.

By talking about our trauma, we are processing all those emotions that were stifled when we were going through the experience.

How many of you describe your response to D-Day as shock? Or say, "I felt numb"?

I know that I somehow got myself dressed, out of the house and managed to make chit-chat with the other moms while picking up my kids. It was like some weird out-of-body experience. I could watch myself making small talk and smiling at the teachers and pretending with my kids that everything was A-okay.

That, my friends, is a trauma response. That is survival instinct kicking in. And it's helpful. It's helpful to ensure that children get picked up from school, that dinner gets put on the table, that jobs get done, that life goes on. But, over the long term, it's not helpful, it's harmful.

It produces post-trauma. It might show up as a numbness that simply doesn't go away, even when it becomes safe to process feelings. It might show up as depression, or self-loathing (which is anger turned inward). It might be nightmares. It might be anxiety. It might be an out-of-proportion response to something seemingly benign. Like completely panicking when your husband is five minutes late coming home from work.

I once went berserk when I couldn't reach my husband on the phone and he was at the grocery store. I went ballistic on him. To him, *what was the big deal?* To me, not being able to reach him was EXACTLY what had happened the morning I found out. This wasn't about him being unreachable at the grocery store. This was about me being totally transported back to that awful, horrible morning when my world fell apart. To that consistent 33-second wait while I listened to his phone ring until it went to voicemail. 33 seconds. I watched the clock. Over and over as my brain caught up to what my body had known for weeks.

This was about post-trauma.

And, as Trunk points out, the way to turn post-trauma into PAST trauma is to talk about it.

The key here is *talk*. This isn't about raging and screaming and dredging up every last unkind thing your spouse has ever done. In fact, that won't get you anywhere. It's about telling *your* story. It's about someone bearing witness to your fear and your confusion. It's about someone confirming that this happened. And it was horrible. It's about reminding yourself over and over again, that this happened...*but it's not happening now*.

You survived.

You survived to tell your story.

It can be really tough, however, to convince your husband of this.

You tell your story and he hears, over and over again, I'm a total asshole who did this. I'm a cheating, lying scumbag. No matter that you're not exactly saying that (though you might be thinking it), that's what he hears. And he doesn't WANT to hear that. He doesn't WANT to be reminded of what he did. Who would?

Though a therapist or good friend can also listen to your story, it's often those who created our trauma that we want to listen to our story. We want our husbands to listen to our pain and reassure us that we will never have to go through that again. That it's over. That they are doing everything they can to make sure they never walk down that same path. That they never want to hurt us like that again.

That's it. Most of us don't want our husbands to beat themselves up. We don't want the focus to be on them at all. This is about *us*.

And the opportunity to tell our story, or part of it, each time we're triggered moves us forward. It helps us heal. And each time our husband is able to be with us in that pain, to listen without defending himself, or minimizing our experience, or telling us why we shouldn't feel that way, our marriage is strengthened. We're on the same team, trying to beat back trauma.

But each time we're silenced, told we're "living in the past," told we're hurting ourselves, that we need to let it go and move on, our trauma goes deeper underground and our marriage fractures a bit more. We're on opposing teams, each trying to nurse his/her own wound at the expense of the other.

The story of our betrayal is a key part of who we are. But sharing that story carries with it the power to heal, not only ourselves but our marriages.

U

Uncertainty, How to Cope With

"In truth, we never know our partner as well as we think we do. ...even in the dullest marriages, predictability is a mirage." Esther Perel (see also **Perel, Esther**) wrote that in her book "Mating In Captivity."

I would have told you that my husband would never cheat on me. I suspect you would have said the same thing. With very few exceptions, most of us are absolutely shocked when we discovered our husband's affair. Despite statistics that indicate that more marriages are affected by infidelity than *aren't* affected, we nonetheless think we're among the lucky few.

When we discover the truth, that our spouse, who we thought we knew inside and out, had a life completely apart from us, it threatens everything we believe we know about our world.

Perel suggests that the discovery should be understood as evidence that we can't ever completely know another person.

But, oh, how uncomfortable that is.

Consequently, our culture delivers up a one-size-fits-all response to infidelity that reduces it to caricature. Cheaters are narcissistic Casanovas. Other Women are a cross between Jessica Rabbit and Glenn Close. It disallows nuance from the conversation.

We need to acknowledge, publicly, just how rampant infidelity is – and we need that acknowledgement within the context of a non-judgemental conversation. Not a conversation that says, necessarily, that infidelity is okay; simply a conversation that says it *is*. That says all people who cheat are not bad people. All women who stay with their unfaithful partners are not doormats. And all cheating isn't remedied by throwing the cheater out. Infidelity caricature soothes our fear of uncertainty. Removing the cheater from our lives, the thinking goes, will protect us from future pain. Or removing the cheater from our lives means we won't have to deal with the pain of healing. We won't have to cope with the uncertainty of *will he do it again?* True, perhaps. But the only way to completely protect ourselves is to close our hearts to not just our cheating spouse...but the world.

Life is uncertain. It's messy. It's a truth writ large when we're healing from betrayal.

And by acknowledging that our spouse has parts of him that we don't know, we not only face the possibility of infidelity (again), but we also open ourselves to the pleasure of new. As Perel writes, that compromise we believe we must make in a long-term monogamous relationship – that in order to have the safety of fidelity, we must give up the excitement of the new – isn't necessary. It's possible, she proposes, to have both fidelity and the thrill of new by recognizing that our spouse is constantly evolving. That we don't know everything about him.

It's something a lot of us learn post-infidelity: healing

from betrayal can include the reinvention of the marriage into something exciting and fulfilling. We can see our spouse in a new light. Not always flattering, at least at first. But if we're open to it, we can rediscover our spouse in a way that encourages the rebuilding of our marriage.

That's not to say I'm an advocate for infidelity. The pain it creates is too devastating. The cost to families is too high.

What I am saying is that if we could open ourselves to the recognition that long-term monogamy can be stultifying, that even good spouses can feel deadened by the day-in, day-out demands of marriage and parenthood, we could have that difficult conversation – beyond *if you cheat, I'm outta here* – with a deeper understanding. We can't inoculate ourselves from pain by trying to frighten our spouse into good behaviour.

Being tempted isn't a sign that the marriage is dead. It's a signal that we have needs that require attention. Temptation is a warning to turn back toward our partner. To ask ourselves what we can do to make the long-term partnership (or other parts of our life) more appealing than the lure of a new partner. To make the choice, again and again, to work on what we have rather than risk it for what we don't.

To do this is to face our fear of abandonment, a fear that runs deep in many of us. By talking about infidelity, we don't make it more likely, we make it less likely. Pretending we're immune to it doesn't make it so.

Let's agree that we can't possibly know everything about our spouses. And let's allow that to make us curious about them, not frightened. It requires a leap of faith. But choosing to stay with a spouse who has betrayed us is all about faith. In him, yes. But more importantly, in ourselves.

Having that faith in myself, though, is one of the gifts that arose from the pain of my husband's infidelity. I learned, the hard way, that the only person I can ever really trust is myself. At first that struck me as sad. But a deeper look revealed how liberating that is. I can be the rock upon which I build my life.

And I can open myself to the uncertainty that is everyone else.

V

Vigilance (especially Hyper)

BWC member StillStanding1 wrote this "ultimate guide to dealing with hypervigilance":

We used to be able to trust our eyes and ears. Our brains were reliable tools that operated (so we thought) with objectivity and logic. We could trust our guts, our womanly intuition. And then, suddenly, horrifically, we learn that our senses have not been telling us the truth, have been faulty or offline. Our intuition has been fooling us or maybe we fooled ourselves into not listening to it. Our brains have turned into out-of-control locomotives, racing down the tracks in some dark, unfamiliar land and we are helpless to stop it. We feel crazy. We can't stop thinking about a thousand "what ifs" and "I should have seen this" and mind movies (see also ***Mind Movies****) and "oh my God! Make it stop." And we can't stop crying. Randomly. In the grocery store. Driving to pick up the kids at school. Hearing a song on the radio. We're afraid to watch the TV in case something triggers (see also* ***Triggers****) us. We are standing in the tall grass and we know the lions are coming for us. Suddenly, the whole world is a danger zone.*

Post-infidelity, we become hypervigilant and hypersensitive. Bright lights, loud noises, crowded spaces, everything makes us jump out of our skin or fall to our knees. It is a natural response to such a massive threat to safety. We have been traumatized (see also ***Trauma****) and old reptilian parts of the brain kick in, trying to keep us safe.*

As more details come to light, in a process quaintly dubbed trickle truth (see also ***Trickle Truth****), we attempt to create a narrative that makes sense. When I was with our daughter at the nephrologist, trying to determine why a 16-year-old would have kidney stones, you were on a "business trip." When you were in the basement playing that song, it wasn't for me.*

We start looking for clues everywhere. We turn into sleuths, searching online, on their phones, asking questions, checking in, examining credit card and phone bills, installing questionable tracking apps (see also ***Spyware****). We start analyzing every word, every facial expression. Did he blink and look left? Was what he just said true? What did he leave out? What is he hiding? Why didn't he check in when he said he would? What doesn't add up? We scour books and articles for any clues that might tell us what the hell is happening and how to make it stop. And we think and worry and think and worry and brace for impact. We don't want to be fooled again. We are constantly on watch. Constantly alert to the possibility of more lies and deception. We don't sleep. We don't eat. It's not sustainable. All these activities, all the sleuthing wears us out and gets in the way of taking care of ourselves. Our instinct is fight or flight. But if we are constantly scanning the horizon for new threats, we can't slow down and listen to what our bodies, our gut, is telling us about right now.*

Tuning into ourselves is the first step toward stopping the crazy train of hypervigilance. How? Be still and take slow, deep breaths. Pause. Note what is happening (my heart is pounding, I'm sweating, I'm panicking). Label it. When you give the thing a name, you have power over it (and not the other way around). Search for objective evidence before reacting (and if you can't, if you've been triggered, be kind and gentle with yourself about it). Be mindful. Pay attention to what your body is telling you. But to do this, you need to slow down and listen. The final step to working with and through hypervigilance is to set boundaries (see also ***Boundaries****) with the person (or people – I'm looking at you, in-laws of the world) who trigger you.*

Boundaries are about what you will and will not tolerate. It's a way to hold ourselves and others accountable for acting with integrity and treating us with respect. Boundaries work best when you are clear on the consequences if certain lines are crossed. Boundaries take the place of hypervigilance because they do the same job. They keep an eye on things but with boundaries, you can eat, or take a nap, or run, or visit friends, or meditate because boundaries will be on duty, so you don't have to be.

Recently, I had another little rumble with over-thinking and hypervigilance. I got more information (note: trickle truth, above). It was disappointing, more deception revealed, and it made me wonder: Was I over-thinking? Did he mean what I think he meant or did I misunderstand? Is he really that manipulative? Is it on purpose? Is my bias now leading me to see everything as evidence for the conclusions I have already drawn? And I see this over-thinking playing out in a cycle of depression and losing the threads of my self-care regimen. I'm tired so I make less time for running, so I eat poorly, so I feel tired, so I make less time for the gym, so I start to feel less worthy and stress about my weight, so I eat poorly so I feel too tired or sad to work out. It's a doom loop.

Once I notice, I can pause, note that I am over-thinking and try to bring myself back to the present. Right now, I am okay. Right now, I am breathing. Right now, I have a roof over my head and enough to eat. Right now, there are people who love me. Right now, I can choose to go for a walk. Right now, I can soak in the tub, take a multivitamin, eat an apple, call a friend. I can make a choice that puts my care and feeding first.

Because ultimately, all the FBI-level, hypervigilance in the world isn't going to stop a person from cheating, if they choose to do so. It isn't going to stop us from being hurt in the future (because newsflash! if you are alive and human, life is going to be both amazing and painful, sometimes at the same time). It isn't going to change the past, no matter how much we wish it would. We can only, in the end, control ourselves. When we stop trying to control those who have hurt us, we release ourselves from so much suffering.

It's hard. You'll stumble. You might have a good day and then suddenly notice on a walk that you are 15 minutes into rehearsing a rant at the OW. It's okay. Here's your opportunity. Pause. Breathe. Notice. Breathe. Label. Breathe. Let it go. Breathe.

Elle's note: I'll add that hypervigilance can be the product of trauma and sometimes requires more intensive therapy. If your hypervigilance is accompanied by tunnel vision, tingling, a profound sense of dread or other trauma symptoms, please reach out for professional help.

W

Wait (see also Rest)

You do not need to decide rightthisminute what you are going to do about your husband, about your marriage, about anything. Sometimes the best thing you can do is give yourself permission to wait. To wait until you have more information. To wait until your panic disorder is under control. To wait until you've saved up some money. To wait until you have a better job. You don't have to wait, of course. But you can.

"Where Do We Begin" Podcast (See also Perel, Esther)

Perel made the jump from books to podcast and her "Where Do We Begin" series gives us fly-on-the-wall access to the secrets of other people's marriages. Perel doesn't always feature couples who've experienced infidelity, but even those who haven't are wrestling with problems that many of us face. It's definitely worth downloading and listening. Perel's insight and compassion helps us all.

WICKED BIBLE, THE

Is it possible our husbands, at least the ones who consider themselves God-fearing Christians, got their hands on a copy of what's been dubbed "The Wicked Bible"? "Wicked" because it offers up this as the Seventh Commandment: Thou Shalt Commit Adultery. Admittedly these bibles, printed in 1631, are in short supply. The rather breathtaking error was discovered a year after publication and the monarch at the time, King Charles, ordered every copy retrieved and reduced to ashes. Somehow, however, 11 copies survived. This commandment to lay down with another man's wife, however, wasn't the only error in this tome. In Deuteronomy 5:24, a passage that, in other editions proclaims the "greatness" of God, instead proclaims a divine "great-asse." Wicked, yes. Wickedly funny.

X

EXit Plan (see also Escape Plan)

Every now and then a woman arrives at the Betrayed Wives Club with a story of betrayal that is a bit different than most. In these stories, the infidelity has been flaunted. Used by the husband as a way to humiliate his wife. This is abuse. Though I rarely tell any betrayed wife whether I think she should stay or go (we each walk our own path to healing), in cases like this, I strongly urge women to leave. If leaving was easy, however, they likely would have done it by now. Enter an Exit Plan. An Exit Plan (see also **Escape Plan**) is a longer-term plan that creates options that don't exist right now. For instance, an Exit Plan might include an appointment with someone who works with abused women to help them mentally prepare to leave. It might mean getting a diploma or degree in order to be able to get a good job and become financially independent. It might mean developing stronger friendships outside of the marriage or pursuing interests that have languished. It should include refusing unprotected sex with your husband. It should also include a personal bank account that holds money he has no access to.

If infidelity in your marriage is being used as a way of undermining your self-esteem, of keeping you destabilized within your marriage, as a way of exerting power, then you are in an abusive relationship. Exit.

X, Mark with

Here's your plan for self-care. It's only a template. You can create your own, focussed on those things that fill you back up when the world has emptied you.

Physical self-care:
Am I eating well?
Am I exercising my body?
Am I allowing myself time to rest?
Am I attending to medical needs?

Emotional self-care:
Am I respecting my boundaries? (see also **Boundaries**)
Am I nurturing healthy relationships with friends?
Am I giving myself time for activities that soothe me (reading, music, crafts, journaling)?

Spiritual self-care:
Am I meditating?
Am I spending time in nature?
Am I feeding my soul (religious services, secular pursuits, inspirational reading)?
Do I take note of what I'm grateful for each day?
Do I have volunteer activities that connect me to those less fortunate than I?

Professional self-care:

Can I find the value in the work I perform?

Am I ensuring a healthy balance between paid and unpaid work?

Social self-care:

Am I spending time in activities with people who share my values?

Am I seeking situations that remind me to laugh?

Financial self-care:

Am I spending money on things that align with my values and goals?

Am I saving money to create security and the freedom to make choices?

Have I created a budget to balance wants/needs?

Psychological self-care:

Do I have a therapist who I trust to help me heal?

Am I making sure to take time away from electronic devices?

Your self-care team:

Do I have an emergency self-care plan for when I'm in crisis:

•Someone I can call who will help me without judgement

•An app on my phone to help me breathe when I'm triggered

•Crisis line

Y

You are here

.

First you were there (at the beginning of this book) and, if you read this front to back, you are now here. And you're different than you were. That's the thing with betrayal. We tell ourselves that we will "never" get over this pain. That we will "always" be sad. Those are lies. We move through life, shifting in ways so small we often don't see it.

Each day, you are getting stronger. You are getting clearer on your Next Right Step (see also **Next Right Step**). You are becoming more certain that you will survive this, except for the days when you're certain you won't. But I, and so many others who've made it through betrayal, know you will. The answer to the rest of your life is

Yes.

Z

Zzzzzzzzs, When You're Not Getting Enough

The worst thing in the world is to try to sleep and not to. -F. Scott Fitzgerald

F. Scott Fitzgerald, something of a philanderer himself, clearly knew a thing or two about insomnia. And infidelity, in a clear case of life imitating art. Or vice versa.

Those of us dealing with betrayal know the endless agony of a restless night.

I would start feeling anxious about sleep hours before I actually went to bed. I would issue a silent prayer to the Gods of Betrayed Wives to please, *please* let me fall asleep and *stay that way*.

Inevitably, I would wake around 3:30 a.m. with a sudden, wide-eyed dread. And I would stay awake. My mind, to paraphrase beloved author Anne Lamott, is like a bad neighborhood. You don't want to go there when it's dark. And – *ohhhh* – was it dark.

It would whisper awful things to me. About how hideous I was. How unlovable. Night unleashes the dark dogs.

I was making a strong effort to steer clear of alcohol, barely trusting myself sober to stay on this side of the law and certainly not willing to tempt fate by climbing into a bottle of merlot. So that sleep-inducing option was out. I tried various teas. But my particular insomnia needed the big guns. I leaned temporarily on a doctor-prescribed sleep aid, on nausea medication with the side-effect of drowsiness, and finally settled on melatonin, a supplement that a flight-attendant friend of mine relies on to adjust her body clock during long-haul flights. Melatonin occurs naturally in our brains – production increases when it becomes dark, signalling to our bodies that it's time for sleep, and increases with light, signalling time to wake.

It worked. It took a week or so for my body to adjust. And the cynic in me wonders if perhaps it was a psychosomatic response to the ritual of taking the capsule. Whatever! I mostly fell asleep and woke up with enough energy to get myself to noon, if not to dinner time, without falling apart.

Zenith

[zee-nith]

Noun

1. The point on the celestial sphere vertically above a given position or observer.
2. A highest point or state; culmination.

I often read the laments of a betrayed wife who misses "the old me." What they (or we) are saying is that they miss the lightness with which they used to live life. They miss the naivety with which they lived, the absolute conviction that they were safe with this partner they'd chosen.

I understand the feelings of loss. I wailed to my husband on more than one occasion that he had "broken me". I imagined myself irrevocably damaged, never again to live with levity, with a faith that the path before me was clear.

I'd outsourced my safety. I'd placed my heart in the hands of a man who, at the time, was unworthy of it. And I'd kept little of my heart for myself. I had no blueprint for self-love. It had always struck me as self-centred, as selfish. Self-love meant less for others, surely.

And so I gave it all away. And I was empty.

Which is why, when I discovered my husband's infidelity, I was so thirsty for evidence that I was loved, that I was worthy, that I was safe. But my well, long forgotten, was dry.

Healing from his cheating was a process of refilling that well. It was a daily practice of self-love, of seeing my own pain and not fleeing from it, of holding it and allowing my soul to grow stronger from it, by feeling it and letting it teach me.

Healing from his cheating was about letting the rain fall and knowing that water was being collected to nourish me in some profound way. And that, when the sun came out again – and I was slowly believing that it would – that the collected rain would be enough to quench my thirst again.

Healing from his affair was about letting go of fantasies about the old me. It's about honouring her, about grieving her, about saluting how hard she tried, how brave she was. But it's about realizing that the old me has grown muscles in her soul that weren't there before, or at least, hadn't been tapped.

New me = old me + pain x wisdom.

That lightness inside can become a light inside that can illuminate the path for others still to come, who will learn from what we've learned, who will heal from our healing, who will gain strength from our strength.

This is how we heal. By loving ourselves and then extending that love outward but always making sure there's water in our well for when we thirst.

We might not have reached our zenith. But that's where we're heading.

Acknowledgments

Thank-you to the legions of women who bring their pain to Betrayed Wives Club and transform it into support and healing for others. In particular, my secret sisterhood is so much richer for Steam, StillStanding1, Phoenix, Iris, Theresa, Lynn Less Pain, Beach Girl, Trying Hard, Hopeful30, the various Sams, the many Anns, and all the others whose online IDs I've forgotten but whose words and kindness I have not.

Made in the USA
Monee, IL
24 April 2022

95346336R00105